DANCE
IN
SARATOGA SPRINGS

DANCE
IN SARATOGA SPRINGS

DENISE WARNER LIMOLI

THE History PRESS

Published by The History Press
Charleston, SC 29403
www.historypress.net

Cover images courtesy of Maurice Seymour, the Saratoga Performing Arts Center and Steve J. Nealy.

First published 2013

Manufactured in the United States

ISBN 978.1.60949.167.3

Library of Congress CIP data applied for.

Mae G. Banner
(1933–2007)

Photo courtesy of Shawn Banner.

Art is not supposed to be a commodity you sell. Art is something that a civil society must support.
—Mae Banner through her son, Shawn

Mae Banner loved dance. She cherished words and understood their power. She believed in advocating for, indeed fighting for, something that was important to her and to her community.

Mae also loved Saratoga Springs. She attended every local dance performance she could, whether or not she was allowed to write about it. Her support of the dance community in Saratoga Springs must not be underestimated. Mae was always there.

Dance in Saratoga Springs *is dedicated to the memory of Mae G. Banner, with the gratitude of the entire Saratoga dance community for her unwavering appreciation and support.*

Contents

Acknowledgements

The following people were interviewed or gave assistance during the preparation and research process. I am grateful for their participation.

Saratoga Dance Teachers

Oleg Briansky/Mireille Briane, Briansky Saratoga Ballet Center
Peggy Delay, Stepping Star School of Dance and Gymnastics
Phyllis Latin, American Dance Center
Dianne Carola, Dance Factory
Aggie Jacobowsky, for Michael Steele, Ballet Regent
Julie Gedalecia, Saratoga City Ballet (Patricia Pugh Moore)
Christie Handley, School of the Arts, National Museum of Dance
Leslie Anne LaGuardia, Arthur Murray International
Beth Fecteau, Nacre Dance Company
Raul Martinez, Director School of the Arts, National Museum of Dance
David Otto, Saratoga Ballet Academy, former NYCB
Robert Maiorano, miscellaneous schools, teacher, author, actor, former NYCB

Skidmore College Dance Faculty

Isabel Brown, faculty emerita, Skidmore dance historian
Mary DiSanto-Rose, associate professor of dance, dance advocate
Debra J. Fernandez, professor and chair of dance, choreographer

Skidmore College Special Programs

Donald McCormack, former dean of Special Programs and dance advocate
Sharon Arpey, director of programs, institutes and conferences
Antoinette (Toni) Smith, faculty advisor

Saratoga Performing Arts Center (SPAC)

Mrs. Kay Leach, wife of Richard Leach, first director of SPAC
Edward Lewi, former owner Ed Lewi Associates, SPAC Board of Directors
Lisa Hill, director of public relations
Marcia White, artistic director and president of SPAC
Ronald Riggi, SPAC Board of Directors, local businessman

National Museum of Dance

Mrs. Marylou Whitney, founder and original president
Carol and Edward Swyer, father was founder Lewis Swyer, Board of Directors SPAC and National Museum of Dance
Alison Moore, first director
Sharon Walsh, initial volunteer, assistant to Ms. Moore; executive assistant to Marcia White, SPAC
Heather Mabee, former president
Michele Riggi, current president
Donna Skiff, current director

New York City Ballet (NYCB)

Peter Martins, ballet master in chief
Erin Hestvik, archivist
Justin Peck, dancer and choreographer
Ellen Sorin, director, The Balanchine Trust
Kathryn Levy, NYCB Education Department
Daniel Duel, former dancer and musician

New York State Summer Schools of the Arts (NYSSSA)

Mary Daly, director emerita
Carolyn Adams, director, School of Modern Dance

Saratoga Springs

Mary Ann Fantauzzi, high school teacher, Dance Alliance president, owner of Total Body Trifecta, dance education advocate, For Arts Sake
Rhona Koretzky-Forman, former librarian, dance fan and advocate, For Arts Sake.
Leslie Roy-Heck, owner Saratoga Dance and Bunheads, former dancer NYCB, Board of Directors National Museum of Dance
Susan Edwards, programming director, National Museum of Dance, dance fan
Shawn Banner, son of Mae Banner, artist and dance advocate
Jay Rogoff, poet and dance writer, Skidmore College
Kim Vanyo, designer for fashion and costuming, owner Khymanyo Studio
Michael Limoli, ballet pianist and clarinetist, former dancer
Carl Landa, dance musician, composer
Sheila Parkert, former owner Adelphi Hotel and dance fan
Peter Kobor, friend of Zachary Solov, theater manager, designer
Andrew Wentink, archivist and librarian, Middlebury College, dance historian

Saratoga Springs History

Mary Ann Fitzgerald, Saratoga Springs city historian
Field Horne, local historian
Mayor Raymond Watkin, former mayor of Saratoga Springs and ballet fan
Terri Blasko, Saratoga Room, Saratoga Library
John Connors, Bolster Collection, Saratoga Springs Historical Society

Introduction

Ballet has been my calling for over fifty years. As a professional dancer, ballet master, choreographer and teacher, I have experienced all aspects of my profession. When the request for this book came to me, I immediately accepted, trusting that I knew enough about the topic. I expected it would be a relatively easy task, but that was only partially correct.

While beginning my research on the evolution of dance in Saratoga Springs, I discovered a multilayered story that involved countless interesting people. It was then that I decided on the "right" method for me: direct contact with as many of these fascinating people as possible. These interviews took place over fourteen months; some were face-to-face and some via e-mail or telephone.

I was humbled by stories of those visionaries who were the driving force at the beginning of the Saratoga Performing Arts Center. Former New York City Ballet dancers entertained me with their tales of Saratoga. I felt pride in the growth of dance at Skidmore College and in the successes of the National Museum of Dance. Mostly, I was touched by the enthusiasm, love and support of the Saratoga dance fans.

Saratoga Springs continues to attract talented artists who lend a special vibrant sophistication to the community. Dancers and those who love them are an important part of the cultural fabric of our city. It is my hope that the local support and enthusiasm I have learned so much about will continue so that the beauty of dance will thrive in Saratoga Springs for future generations.

Thanks to my husband, Michael Limoli, and daughter, Francesca Limoli, for their patience while reading and helping to edit my work. I especially want to thank all the wonderful people who gave me their time and shared their memories during interviews. They helped guide me through the process and generated further contacts. The list of names is long, and it demonstrates that these people themselves are the story of dance in Saratoga Springs.

Chapter 1

Entertainment in Nineteenth-Century Saratoga Springs

Early in the nineteenth century, Saratoga Springs began developing its natural mineral springs into what would become the city's world-renowned spa facilities. Saratoga subsequently became the summer destination for America's elite society, which was familiar with the great spas of Europe. Known as the "Queen of Spas," Saratoga Springs offered visitors the natural beauty of the surroundings and the health benefits of the mineral waters. Its summer guests enjoyed elegant accommodations in opulent hotels and a variety of entertainments, including evening balls and gambling. Members of the great American families, international celebrities, business tycoons and politicians all came to Saratoga Springs for the summer spa season.

The hotels were famous. Union Hall, built by the Putnam family as a boardinghouse in 1802, evolved into the Grand Union Hotel, the world's largest hotel and one of the most opulent. Along with the Grand Union, the United States Hotel and Congress Hall composed an elegant trio with grand piazzas on Broadway where guests would promenade and enjoy musical entertainment.

One of the earliest entertainers in the village was Mr. Vilallave, a traveling player who performed acrobatics on the tightrope and sleight of hand magic tricks. Vilallave remained in Saratoga, where he erected a small playhouse. This was replaced in 1821 by a more substantial theater on the corner of Washington and Federal Streets, known popularly as "Vilallave's Theatre."

Announcement of an appearance by Vilallave. *Collection of the Saratoga Springs city historian.*

The Hop at Congress Hall. *Collection of the Saratoga Springs city historian.*

As Saratoga grew, other small playhouses and lecture halls were built, many to be adapted later by emerging religious congregations. The 1848 St. Nicholas Hall on Broadway at Phila Street was considered the "most sumptuous playhouse of the time." Over the next forty years, several large theaters were constructed. The Leland Opera House, a grand theater that could seat 1,600, was erected on the park-like grounds of the Grand Union Hotel. The Congress Hall Ballroom opened in the 1870s, and the largest public space of all, the Convention Hall, had a seating capacity of 5,000.[1]

With the growing popularity of gambling, the tradition of the annual summer visit to the spa soon gave way to horse racing and casinos. Harness racing was overshadowed by the Thoroughbreds when the Saratoga Race Course opened in 1864. The elegant Morrissey's Club House was built in Congress Park and later renamed the Canfield Casino. Several lake houses with fine restaurants and casinos were built along Saratoga Lake to accommodate the demand for high-stakes gambling in Saratoga Springs.[2]

SARATOGA'S FLORAL FÊTES

In 1893, a group of concerned local citizens came together to discuss projects that could extend the duration of the summer season and repair the city's reputation, which was being tarnished by gambling. They chose the Floral Fête, and a Floral Association was established and charged with organizing the festival.

In September 1894, Saratoga's first Floral Fête debuted, complete with a parade down Broadway of carriages and floats decorated with thousands of beautiful flowers. Over three thousand people attended the first grand Floral Ball, an elegant entertainment of music and dance in the Convention Hall.[3] This performance featured several ballets danced by beautifully costumed young women and children. Mr. Meredith Stanton Frothingham, who was the master of ceremonies at the United States Hotel, staged the Dance of the Roses and Butterflies. Mr. Jacob Mahler arranged the Waltz of the Flowers for a large group of children, including soloist Miss Rosalind Mahler, whose "dancing enhanced by the efforts of the other children, elicited considerable applause. It was her last farewell to the Saratoga public for the season."[4]

The Saratoga Floral Fêtes continued annually for almost a decade. Each year, the festivals became more elaborate and attracted hundreds of thousands of tourists who traveled to Saratoga Springs in specially decorated train cars. The parades added bicycles, children's prams and eventually motorcars, all covered with beautiful flowers and greenery. All the buildings along Broadway were festooned with greenery and blossoms. In 1900, elaborate floats were imported directly from New Orleans' Mardi Gras celebrations. The lavish Rex Pageant and the Proteus Pageant were introduced, and for the next several years the festival expanded to four days.[5]

The Floral Ball also evolved with more complex productions based on a different theme each year. The theme of the third festival was "Arcticania," which was described thus:

> *It was a poet's dream ably and beautifully depicted, with all the grace and charm that surrounds childhood and womanhood. For an hour, frost maidens, snowflakes, snow elves and icicles held sway among flowers and forests of evergreens...and the luminous Polar Star gorgeous in attire, appeared among them. The star, Miss Margaret Tynan of New York was a vision of loveliness in a costume of white gauze, a star of diamonds on her head and a drapery of all over silver tissue from neck to waist.*[6]

Children in costume for the 1899 Floral Fête. *Saratoga Room Collection, Saratoga Springs Public Library, photo by Epier.*

"The Realm of Roses," "Columbia," "Le Mer" and "Flora's Retenne" were the themes of subsequent Floral Balls, all staged by Mr. Frothingham. Other popular dancers of the day included "Miss Mae C. Bennett, a twelve year old toe dancer from Troy, and Saratoga's Miss Daphna Leonard Chase, a fourteen year old ballerina who was a student of Professor Van Arnum."[7]

The phenomenon of Saratoga's Floral Fêtes eventually ended in 1905 due to a gradual decline in public interest and mounting financial losses. The Floral Association dissolved two years later, citing "too much of a good thing" as one of the problems.[8]

Twentieth-Century Vaudeville and Pageants

Although gambling had been declared illegal, it was still very popular in the summer lake houses. These establishments had their own orchestras

Meadowbrook Lake House dancers. *Bolster Collection, Saratoga Springs Historical Society.*

and dancers, and famous vaudeville performers entertained the clientele. The Meadow Brook Lake House, Neuman's Lake House and Riley's Lake House were some of the most successful and regularly attracted wealthy patrons every summer. The Saratoga casinos eventually became linked with infamous gangsters, and by the 1950s, lake house gambling was shut down by the state.[9]

In town, the remaining local theaters were now venues for popular vaudeville acts. Dancers in these acts were entertaining at best or considered risqué at worst. However, in the early twentieth century, there were some performers who brought a new style of dance to the public. Inspired by the revolutionary dancer Isadora Duncan, an interpretive style of dance was emerging, later to be named modern dance.

In the summer of 1914, the famous dancer Ruth St. Denis and her partner, Ted Shawn, were married in Saratoga Springs. The Denishawn ensemble performed at the Canfield Casino on August 19 for an audience of five hundred.[10] Ruth St. Denis was billed as the "World Famous Oriental Dancer," and she and Shawn performed the exotic dances "The Hindoo Snake Charmer" and "The Peacock."[11]

The Spa Little Theatre was built as part of a government-funded initiative to develop the state reservation lands in Saratoga Springs. The 1930s building

Denishawn: Ruth St. Denis and Ted Shawn in *Algerian Dance.* Walter Terry, *The Dance in America.* (New York: Harper and Row, 1971).

The Ballet Russe de Monte Carlo produced Massine's ballet *Saratoga* in 1941. Alexandra Danilova and Frederic Franklin were featured as a young jockey and his sweetheart. Oliver Smith's scenic design was inspired by the Saratoga Race Course. *Photo by Maurice Seymour.*

project included a complex of bathhouses and administrative offices. The Spa Little Theatre began as a medical lecture hall but has evolved into one of the city's primary performance venues for modern dance, opera, chamber music and regional theater.[12]

The Saratoga County Fair flourished during the patriotic 1940s. In addition to exhibits of livestock and produce, popular entertainment was important to lift everyone's spirits. On the vaudeville stage, the revue "Salute to Freedom featured a flock of the world's most beautiful girls dancing in gorgeous gowns specially designed for this production."[13]

In the 1950s, the Saratoga Day Lily Festival was introduced. Reminiscent of the Floral Fêtes, this new festival was another effort to repair the city's reputation and boost local morale. The Katrina Trask Garden Club and the Civic League sponsored the festival that marked the 150th anniversary of Congress Park. Mr. John H. MacGregor was the author and director of a lavish historical pageant performed outside in Congress Park. Dozens of young women danced and sang in honor of Flora, the Queen of Saratoga Springs, and her court.[14]

Dance as entertainment has been documented in Saratoga Springs since the early 1800s. Dance as performance art came later. Skidmore College, serious dance teachers and, eventually, the Saratoga Performing Arts Center are segments of the whole picture. All these components are intertwined in the developing story of dance in Saratoga Springs.

Chapter 2
Skidmore College Dance Department

Miss Lucy Scribner began *The Young Women's Industrial Club of Saratoga Springs* in 1903. The school offered girls a curriculum that included courses in fields that were considered acceptable for young women at that time. They studied typing, book keeping, textile arts and music, and the girls learned folk dances in physical education class. This secondary school was renamed the Skidmore School of Arts in 1911. Dancing in the style of Isadora Duncan was particularly popular, and dancers were featured in the May Day festivals and other celebrations.

Skidmore College for women opened its downtown campus in 1922. By the 1950s, the campus had extended to over eighty buildings on Circular Street, Union Avenue and several side streets. Dance was still an informal physical education activity that took place in the gymnasium.

The college presented visiting dance artists at some of its public events. In 1929, Ruth St. Denis and Ted Shawn performed at a benefit for Skidmore College sponsored by the Physical Education Club.[15]

During the 1950s, the Skidmore Music Series presented a performance of the José Limón Dance Company, and the Skidmore Dance Club presented Martha Myers in the Spa Little Theatre.[16]

Skidmore's "new campus" was constructed on a one-thousand-acre property that was deeded to the college by trustee J. Erik Jonsson. Groundbreaking began in 1963, and by 1968, much of the new campus was functional. The current coeducational campus opened in 1971, and soon after it included a studio facility designated especially for dance.[17]

May Day celebration dancers, 1930s. *Bolster Collection, Saratoga Springs Historical Society.*

SKIDMORE DANCE PROGRAM BEGINS

Dance was incorporated into the academic curriculum in 1969. The first full-time dance faculty member was Isabel Brown, a Vassar College alumna with an MS from Smith College. Professor Brown had training in ballet, modern dance and the south Indian classical dance form Bharatanatyam. Jody Lunt was engaged as a part-time dance teacher. Dance classes took place in the Regent Street gymnasium and in the Lake Avenue Armory building. Initially, only modern dance was taught, but in 1971 Isabel Brown introduced courses in classical ballet, Bharatanatyam, jazz and dance history.

Although dance was still included in physical education, the dance major was established the following year. Students majoring in dance chose from three areas of concentration: General Dance, Pre-Professional Dance Therapy and Teaching. During this period, two renowned modern dancers from the Martha Graham Dance Company, Mary Hinkson and Ethel Winter, taught as guest artists.

Notable among the first dance alumnae are Lila York (1970), Jeanne Bresciani (1972) and Robert Tracy (1977). Ms. York is a former principal dancer with the

Paul Taylor Dance Company. She travels internationally staging Taylor's work and choreographs for major ballet and modern dance companies. Ms. Bresciani is the founder and director of the Isadora Duncan International Institute and travels around the world to lecture and perform. She has maintained a close relationship with the Skidmore Dance Department. The late Robert Tracy performed with Rudolf Nureyev and Friends in New York City, and he maintained a life-long friendship with Mr. Nureyev. Tracy was a well-respected dance writer whose work appeared in *Vanity Fair*, the *New York Times* and other publications. Robert Tracy authored three books on dance: *Balanchine's Ballerinas: Conversations with the Muses* (Simon and Schuster, 1983); *Goddess: Martha Graham's Dancers Remember* (Limelight, 1987); and *Ailey Spirit: The Journey of an American Dance Company* (Limelight, 2004).[18]

Professor Isabel Brown, the first dance faculty member. *Photo by Emma Dodge Hanson.*

Building a Dance Faculty and a Curriculum

Everyone in the dance profession knew that Saratoga Springs was the summer home of the New York City Ballet. There was also a growing awareness of Skidmore College and its developing dance program. This was due in part to the caliber of the college's guest artists and Oleg Briansky's popular summer ballet school.

In 1973, Skidmore College added a famous name to the faculty, and the professional dance community really took notice. Melissa Hayden, the preeminent ballerina from the New York City Ballet, joined the dance faculty after receiving an honorary doctorate from Skidmore College. In her studio on Broadway, she taught Balanchine technique to Skidmore students, as well as public ballet classes and a BOCES program for talented schoolchildren. Ms. Hayden also initiated the Skidmore Dance Month, a summer intensive program offering ballet with Ms. Hayden, Ole Fatum (Denmark) and Juan Anduze (Puerto Rico); modern dance with Paul Sanasardo; and Bharatanatyam with Isabel Brown. She insisted on professional-quality pianists in the studios and brought in Robert Ashby from New York City and Russian pianist Leo Kakurin for ballet and Ralph Gilbert for modern classes. Melissa Hayden left Skidmore in 1976.

In what was originally the athletic field house, a new dance facility opened in 1975. The dance faculty now had two large, state-of-the-art studios with very high ceilings, sprung floors, full mirrors, grand pianos, two small offices and dressing rooms. Performances were occasionally held in the adjoining gym that was adapted with a portable stage and lighting. At that time, the only theater on campus was a temporary space built adjacent to the gymnasium. This intimate "black box" was used by the Theater Department while the much larger Janet Kinghorn Bernhard Theater was being built.

Skidmore ballet dancers in the studio. *Photo by Steve J. Nealey.*

That temporary building is still very much in use and has evolved into the Skidmore Dance Theater. Administered solely by the Dance Department, the Skidmore Dance Theater has enabled the department to offer forty to fifty dance performances per year on its own stage.

A new assistant professor of dance, Elisabeth Carroll, joined the faculty in 1976. She was well known in the profession as an important dancer and a particularly fine ballet teacher; again, the dance world was impressed with Skidmore College. Trained in France and Monte Carlo, Elisabeth Carroll had performed as a soloist with the American Ballet Theatre and later became a principal dancer with the Harkness Ballet. Her husband, Felix Smith, also joined the faculty and taught jazz, partnering and choreography. In addition, Smith served as production manager for performances. During the January term, Elisabeth Carroll and a select group of ballet students traveled to Monte Carlo to study at the Princess Grace Academy of Ballet.

Moss Cohen, another well-known dancer from the prestigious Martha Graham Dance Company, joined the modern dance faculty in 1980. Cohen introduced the dynamic Graham technique to the curriculum. Mary DiSanto-Rose, PhD and DEd from Temple University, joined in 1981. She specialized in two diverse areas: dance education for the young child and staging the works of modern dance pioneers, such as Doris Humphrey and José Limón.

Mary DiSanto-Rose, associate professor of dance. *Photo by Emma Dodge Hanson.*

With a faculty of strong technique teachers in both ballet and modern dance, Skidmore dancers progressed rapidly. Kenneth Topping was a student who discovered dance at Skidmore with Professors Brown, DiSanto-Rose and Cohen. After graduating in 1984, Topping went on to perform for many years as a principal dancer with the Martha Graham Dance Company. He then led the Graham Ensemble and served as the director of the Martha Graham School.[19]

During this period, dance was a program of the Department of Exercise Science, Dance and Athletics. The dance program was integrated into the college-wide curriculum by offering courses in liberal studies, non-Western studies and arts requirements. These courses expanded the reach of dance to hundreds of students across the campus. "Stravinsky and Balanchine: Union of the Minds" was a course introduced by Isabel Brown and Isobel Williams. Professor Charles Joseph, an expert on the work of Igor Stravinsky, later joined Isabel Brown to teach this course. Several New York City Ballet dancers were brought to campus to speak about their firsthand experiences working with Balanchine and Stravinsky. Another liberal studies course, "Women, Creativity and the Performing Arts," was taught by Mary DiSanto-Rose, Carolyn Anderson and Wilma Hall. Dance contributed to the non-Western curriculum with classical Indian dance and African dance forms. The majority of dance technique classes fulfilled the new all-college arts requirement.

Moss Cohen left Skidmore in 1987, and Antoinette (Toni) Smith, MFA in dance from Temple University, was added to the modern dance faculty. She specialized in a very different style of modern dance, and she introduced release technique, somatics and body-mind centering.

Isabel Brown had served as coordinator of dance from 1978 to 1990. Mary DiSanto-Rose became the first director of the dance program in 1990, which gave dance more autonomy, although it was still a part of the Department of Exercise Science, Dance and Athletics. Both Mary DiSanto-Rose and Antoinette Smith were active in dance advocacy organizations and panels, and they had a network of contacts and growing influence in dance in upstate New York.[20]

Felix Smith retired in 1991 and was replaced by Debra Fernandez. Professor Fernandez had already built a reputation as a choreographer for dance and theater. She was known locally as a jazz teacher for both the Briansky summer program and the New York State Summer School of the Arts. Originally a theater student, Debra Fernandez began her dance study at the University of South Florida, where she earned a BA in dance. In addition to teaching both jazz and ballet, she taught choreography and a course in music for dance.

Elisabeth Carroll retired from Skidmore in 1992. Another experienced ballet professional from the American Ballet Theatre, Denise Warner Limoli then joined the department. She was previously on the ballet faculty

Right: Debra J. Fernandez, professor of dance. *Photo by Emma Dodge Hanson.*

Below: Denise Warner Limoli, associate professor of dance. *Photo by Emma Dodge Hanson.*

Mary Harney, artist in residence. *Photo by Emma Dodge Hanson.*

of the University of Cincinnati College-Conservatory of Music and the North Carolina School of the Arts. Professor Limoli focused on rigorous training and on expanding Skidmore's ballet curriculum to include courses in pointe, character dance, men's technique, pas de deux, repertoire and ballet pedagogy.

This decade produced many successful alumni, including Eric Handman (1991). After graduating from Skidmore, Mr. Handman performed with Doug Varone and Dancers, Nicholas Leichter and other modern choreographers. He earned an MFA from the University of Utah, where he is now an assistant professor of modern dance.

Mary Harney joined the modern dance faculty as an artist in residence in 2000. Ms. Harney received a BFA in dance from SUNY Purchase. A native of Schenectady, she taught previously at Union College and for the New York State Summer School of the Arts. At Skidmore, Ms. Harney teaches modern technique, beginning ballet and choreography and is a prolific choreographer for dance concerts.

In the spring of 2007, Isabel Brown, Skidmore's first dance professor, retired. Professor Brown was celebrated by a large gathering of dance alumni and colleagues. In the Spring Dance Concert, guest artists from the American Ballet Theatre appeared with the students of the Classical Ballet Workshop in *Swan Lake, Act II*, danced in Professor Brown's honor.

Isabel Brown had been a constant driving force in dance at Skidmore College. In her own words, she "worked to establish dance in academe as a liberal arts course of study with its own curriculum, its own complex body of knowledge and its many possible interdisciplinary connections."

After thirty-six years of building the dance curriculum, Professor Brown finally saw her dream of autonomy for dance realized. In 2005, the dance

Rubén Graciani, associate professor of dance. *Photo by Emma Dodge Hanson.*

program left Exercise Science and Athletics and became the independent Department of Dance.

The most recent addition to the dance faculty is Rubén Graciani. Graciani earned an MFA in dance from the University of Maryland–College Park and taught previously at Ohio University in Athens. He was trained at the North Carolina School of the Arts, Juilliard School and SUNY Purchase. Graciani performed professionally with the Mark Morris Dance Company, the Joe Goode Performance Group and Company Stefanie Batten-Bland, among others. At Skidmore College, he has taught modern dance, partnering and choreography. An award-winning choreographer, Rubén Graciani has recently established his own dance company, RG Dance Project, in New York City.[21]

In addition to the studio courses, the dance faculty teaches dance history and the Senior Dance Capstone course. Dance history is taught in a two-course sequence, followed by the first semester of the Dance Capstone course. Students learn research techniques and the specifics of writing for dance in these courses.

The Dance Department offers students unlimited opportunities to create work, which is a major focus of the dance curriculum. Students practice their craft in the improvisation classes and then move into the Choreography

I and II courses. The Senior Dance Capstone course is the final opportunity for the dance major to produce a major work. After graduation, many Skidmore dance alumni have continued their own choreographic projects, and several have taken the big step of starting their own companies.

Although ballet and modern dance technique courses are the foundation of the training curriculum, there are other forms included as well. Ethnic forms such as African and Indian dance, tap and jazz styles, yoga and Pilates courses and anatomy and injury prevention complete the curriculum. These classes are taught by a group of experts such as the master drummer from Ghana, Yacub Ady; Veena Chandra from north India; experienced Broadway performers Debra Pigliavento and Tina Baird; Meghan Del Prete (2002), a Level Five certified instructor in Romana Pilates; and Sarah DiPasquale, a licensed physical therapist who specializes in working with dancers.

One unique aspect of dance at Skidmore College is that all students on campus are able to participate in the department. Any student may enroll in an appropriate level technique class and perform or choreograph alongside the dance majors. The majority of dance majors at Skidmore College pursue another major as well, so the dancers have a variety of influences that enhance their artistic exploration.

Skidmore dancers have excelled in many fields after graduavtion, such as teaching, arts administration, lighting design and physical therapy, as well as performing and choreography. Dancer, choreographer and professor Eric Handman, class of '91, expressed his thoughts on his time at Skidmore College:

> *Without knowing it, I began learning how to teach while learning how to dance at Skidmore. My most memorable teachers were collegial, authentic, grounded, dynamic and undogmatic. They empowered me to uncover, discover and recover myself. What seemed like their knowledge at the time, feels like their wisdom now. They taught with character. Eventually it ignited mine. An enduring lesson from Skidmore: you teach through your character, and your passion gives value to what you teach. The value the Skidmore community placed on making art was just as transformational for me as the art itself. And the importance of being considered a valued member of a meaningful community was the most empowering and life-changing feeling. That experience is what I want for my students. It's in my bones because of my time at Skidmore.*[22]

In addition to the dance faculty, the Department of Dance has a musical staff that plays for ballet and modern dance classes and often performs live in the dance concerts. Musicians Ashby and Kakurin, who came to Skidmore College with Melissa Hayden, both left in the early 1990s. Judith Fitzner Atchinson was the primary modern accompanist when Michael Limoli joined as ballet pianist in 1992. Carl Landa became director of music in 2000 and brought in Patricia Hadfield, Carol Ann Elze-Sussdorff, Adrian Cohen and the late Oleg Moston.

In technical production, Felix Smith and Don Mandigo worked in lighting design and stage management. Lori Dawson, MFA from Amherst College, was a lighting designer in New York City before being hired by Skidmore College in 1998. As the technical director, lighting designer and manager of the Dance Theater, she has developed and greatly improved the dance theater facility. Ms. Dawson created the course Dance Production, a comprehensive course for dancers to learn about lighting design and producing dance performances. Peter Kobor is the stage manager for the Dance Theater and assistant to the technical director. He works concurrently in the Skidmore Theater Department and has designed lighting for dance performances both in the Dance Theater and in the Zankel Music Center. Peter Kobor credits his close friend, the late Zachary Solov, as his mentor in theater arts.

GUEST ARTISTS

Throughout the years, the Skidmore Department of Dance has invited dozens of important professional guest artists to teach technique and to choreograph new work for the students. Some of these artists had already been introduced to Skidmore College through the summer dance residencies of the Office of the Dean of Special Programs. Others were professional colleagues of the dance faculty and were engaged directly by the department. Guest artists visited the dance history classes, and many gave public lectures/demonstrations in the Dance Theater.

The following are only a few of the guest artists who have visited Skidmore College multiple times: Mme. Kirsten Simone, former prima ballerina of the Royal Danish Ballet, taught the unique style of Denmark's August Bournonville and staged several of his ballets. Robert Battle, artistic director of the Alvin Ailey American Dance Company, has staged several of his own pieces for the modern dancers. From India, Shila Mehta, master Kathak dancer and teacher, has enhanced the training of the classical Indian dance students. Two renowned teachers came to campus for one weekend of master classes. In 1993, Savion Glover was obliged to teach his tap master classes in the gym to accommodate the number of dancers. The great jazz teacher Luigi taught dynamic master classes in 2002.

In 1996, the Skidmore Department of Dance began hosting companies in residence during the academic year. This initiative was led by Mary DiSanto-Rose, with financial assistance from the New York State Council on the Arts. The artists stayed on campus for several weeks during the winter break when they could focus on creating new work. Once classes resumed, guests taught technique and choreography classes, gave public performances and presented lecture demonstrations in area schools.

Skidmore dancers had the opportunity to perform with some of the visiting companies. Students appeared with the Pearson/Widrig Dance Theater in their homage to hurricane victims *Katrina, Katrina: Love Letters to New Orleans.* They also performed with David Gordon's Pick Up Performance Company in *Uncivil Wars, Collaborating with Brecht and Eisler*. In 2011, Skidmore dancers joined with the José Limón Dance Company to perform in José Limón's signature works *Missa Brevis* and *There Is a Time.*

DANCE PERFORMANCES

The performances of the Skidmore College Department of Dance are well known for the quality of the dancers and the choreography. Members of the Skidmore College community and regional dance fans regularly attend these sold-out performances in the Skidmore Dance Theater.

The major Winter and Spring Dance Concerts feature a representative array of faculty and guest artist works. The programs showcase either pieces of original choreography or staged classics in modern dance and ballet.

In addition to the works presented by the dance faculty, the modern dancers have performed classics from the Martha Graham and José Limón repertoire and pieces by current guest choreographers such as Robert Battle and Brian Brooks. Ballet dancers have appeared in original works by guests Dwight Rhoden, Peter Pucci and others and have performed excerpts from many of the great nineteenth-century ballets.

There are also informal demonstrations of the work accomplished in a variety of other classes, such as the showings of the classical Indian dance class and the site-specific events of the improvisation classes.

The Senior Dance Capstone course culminates with a series of fully produced performances. In this course, the senior dance majors choose to either choreograph a substantial original work for their peers or to perform a solo choreographed by a contemporary choreographer. Some of the choreographers who have allowed their work to be shown in this course are Lar Lubovich, Kraig Patterson, Leah Cox and Camille A. Brown.

There are two additional venues on campus that allow dance ever-expanding opportunities to collaborate with other artists: the Frances Young Tang Teaching Museum and Art Gallery and the Helen Filene Ladd Concert Hall located in the Arthur Zankel Music Center.

The Tang opened in 2000 and has become a popular venue for both students and faculty to create site-specific dance events. For the museum's grand opening celebration, pianist and former Skidmore College president David Porter and choreographers Mary DiSanto-Rose and Debra Fernandez presented *A Cage/Satie Tang-O*. The artwork of visiting artist Charles Martin and Skidmore's Margo Mensing was featured along with this performance.

Debra Fernandez has since established a strong connection with the Tang through her successful collaborative projects with several of the Tang's featured artists. For the 2002 installation "Elevatious Transcedualistic," by artist Paul Henry Ramirez, she created *Balls*, a dance inspired by the color and movement of the artwork. Ms. Fernandez's piece *Mak3* premiered in 2004. A fascinating work, *Mak3* embodied the Tang's exhibit, "A Very Liquid Heaven," by Skidmore physics professor Mary Crone Odekon and artist Margo Mensing. The 2007 work *Partying* was an avant-garde dance theater piece with dancers in business suits leading the audience throughout the museum as the choreography unfolded. Designer and artist Kim Vanyo created costumes that were inspired by the art exhibits for all of these projects.[23]

The Arthur Zankel Music Center opened in 2010. This award winning concert facility includes a stage with a sprung floor for dance performances and a full-size orchestra pit. A venue of this professional calibre has greatly enhanced the performing and collaborative possibilities for dance, particularly the opportunity for dancers and musicians to perform together.

Both modern dance and ballet have been well represented on the Zankel stage. The first music and dance event was a performance of two pieces by composer Richard Danielpour, who was the 2010 McCormack Visiting

Artist-Scholar in Residence. Choreographer Rubén Graciani presented *A Swing and a Miss* to solo piano, and Debra Fernandez premiered *Swan Song* accompanied by the Hyperion String Quartet. During the fall of 2012, the chamber ensemble ACJW presented Igor Stravinsky's narrated drama *L'Histoire du Soldat* with choreography by Rubén Graciani.

Later that spring, David Porter and Debra Fernandez reunited for an evening of music by John Cage. Artist Margo Mensing and student Brendan Gaffney (2012) created an interactive sound installation throughout the lobby. *Keeping Company with Cage* featured Porter at the prepared piano and Debra Fernandez's choreography for a sophisticated cast of dancers with projected video.

Denise Warner Limoli and conductor Anthony Holland collaborated in 2011 on the first classical ballet produced on the Zankel stage with the full Skidmore Orchestra. *Swan Lake, Act II* was performed by a cast of fifty Skidmore dancers and the sixty-eight-member orchestra.

In April 2013, Professors Warner Limoli and Holland presented *An Evening with the Ballets Russes.* This program featured three ballets from the company's historic repertoire: *Les Sylphides*, *L'Apres Midi d'un Faune* and *Firebird.* Dozens of dancers, a full symphony orchestra, a grand piano, costumes and scenery all came together in an elaborate production that celebrated the Zankel and the artistic collaboration among Skidmore's dancers, musicians and designers.

Skidmore Dancers on Tour

Rubén Graciani has been filming small groups of his dancers at various outdoor locations. His first dance for film, *Rapture*, was a duet shot on a lakeside dock and inside an apartment. The duet *Complete This Work Which We Began* was filmed in a quarry in Schuylerville, and *Terra Arcana* took place in the woods and waters of Lake George. The films challenge viewers to see the possibilities of dance in any location, not just on the stage.[24]

As the reputation of Skidmore's Dance Department grows, the opportunities for dancers to perform off campus have increased. Mary DiSanto-Rose has cultivated a close relationship between Skidmore's dancers and Jeanne Bresciani's Isadora Duncan International Institute. Skidmore dancers have performed and traveled with Ms. Bresciani many times. In 2004 and 2009, Mary DiSanto-Rose and her students accompanied Jeanne Bresciani to Greece, where they studied and

Three Graces choreography by Isadora Duncan. *Photo by Greg Carey.*

performed Duncan's dances in Athens and among the temple ruins of Delphi. The Skidmore Duncan Dancers have also performed in New York City at the 92nd Street Y and at the Kaatsbaan International Dance Center in Tivoli, New York.[25]

Afloat Below the Surface choreography by Rubén Graciani. *Photo by Steve J. Nealey.*

In 2012, Skidmore dancers had the distinct honor of participating in the University Partners Showcase, a festival sponsored by the Martha Graham Dance Company at the Joyce Theater in New York City. Skidmore dancers performed "Steps in the Street" from *Chronicle*, Graham's 1936 commentary on war. Mary Harney worked with representatives of the Martha Graham Dance Company and facilitated this prestigious opportunity.

Rubén Graciani took two Skidmore dancers to New York City to debut his new company, RG Dance Project, and showcase his duet *Afloat Below the Surface* at the Dance/NYC Raw Materials festival at New York University Tisch School for the Arts. They also performed at the Dance Now NYC festival at Joe's Pub, where *Afloat Below the Surface* was voted audience favorite.

In 2012, the entire Spring Dance Concert was performed at Kaatsbaan International Dance Center. This program featured a large cast and included five diverse works by Duncan, Graham, Petipa and Skidmore faculty.

The Skidmore College Department of Dance continues to attract talented students and excellent faculty. Under the leadership of Isabel Brown, Mary DiSanto-Rose and Debra Fernandez, the current chair of dance, this small department in a liberal arts college has grown to national recognition. Skidmore College Department of Dance was recently identified as one of the top five dance schools in the country.[26]

Chapter 3

Saratoga Performing Arts Center and the New York City Ballet Come to Town

"How to Succeed by Really Trying"[27]

Saratoga Springs had lost its luster by the 1950s. The city's influential families and state and civic leaders agreed that something had to be done to reenergize the Capital District. In his editorials, Duane LaFleche of Albany's *Knickerbocker News* suggested that bringing the performing arts to the region would attract tourism and rejuvenate the area.

The concept of building a center for the arts upstate was discussed. Several states had already built outdoor amphitheaters for their orchestras, such as Ravinia in Illinois, Tanglewood in Massachusetts and Aspen Music Festival in Colorado. An ideal location for New York's amphitheater was identified in the State Reservation in Saratoga Springs.

The Saratoga Springs Committee was formed to begin planning this immense project. Inspired by members of the committee, notable racing patrons who made Saratoga their summer home hosted glamorous fundraising parties to spread the word and to generate excitement. Several Thoroughbred horse owners donated stud fees. Local citizens, waiters, teachers, shopkeepers and schoolchildren made small donations so they could be part of this venture. These combined efforts generated a sufficient initial sum to encourage Governor Nelson Rockefeller to release state monies. He was also able to secure additional funding from the Rockefeller family.[28]

The chairman of the Saratoga Springs Committee and first director of the Performing Arts Center, Inc., Newman E. Wait later had this to say about the enthusiasm of the people of Saratoga Springs:

> *As Chairman of the local committee, I am very proud to say that Saratoga residents have already pledged over a quarter-million dollars toward the construction of the Center. This is the best kind of evidence I know to indicate our belief and interest in this cultural venture. I want to thank everyone for their contributions, however great or small.*[29]

The planning committee was responsible for choosing the architectural and construction firms, as well as the performers who would be in residence in the new arts center. One of the early planners from Saratoga Springs was Mr. Robert McKelvey, who worked for the New York State Commerce Department. McKelvey was a self-described balletomane and suggested adding ballet to the programming. He introduced the members of the planning committee to George Balanchine and Lincoln Kirstein of the New York City Ballet. Initially, the New York Philharmonic was invited to be the resident orchestra, but that orchestra declined. However, Maestro Eugene Ormandy and the Philadelphia Orchestra accepted. The decision was soon made that the New York City Ballet and the Philadelphia Orchestra would be the two resident companies of the new eight-week arts festival in Saratoga Springs.

During the design process, Mr. Balanchine, Mr. Kirstein and Maestro Ormandy advised the architects from Vollmer Associates on the requirements for the stage and rehearsal facilities and for the auditorium's acoustics. Groundbreaking began in June 1964, with Governor Nelson Rockefeller driving the tractor. One year later, the L.A. Swyer Construction Company began work building the impressive amphitheater and surrounding buildings.

The first executive director of the Saratoga Performing Arts Center was Richard P. Leach. He had previously established the Aspen Music Festival and had served as program director for Lincoln Center in New York City. Richard Leach was being considered for the executive directorship of the Kennedy Center in Washington, D.C., but he chose to accept the offer from Saratoga Springs. The founding committee had succeeded in securing three world-class partners for the new Saratoga Performing Arts Center: the Philadelphia Orchestra, the New York City Ballet and Mr. Richard Leach.[30] In his speech during the groundbreaking ceremonies, Mr. Leach said:

> *I believe that in the long run this beautiful building will be justified only by the performances which take place in it. We are extremely proud of the performers who have agreed to take part in the first annual Saratoga Festival. The Philadelphia Orchestra and the New York City Ballet rank high among the great performing organizations, not merely of this country, but of the world.*[31]

From the podium, Governor Nelson Rockefeller, who was a great supporter of the arts, was moved to say:

> *I can't help but be impressed and feel strongly that in America, the things that are done, the things that are good, that are exciting, that are wonderful come from the individual creativity and responsibility of free citizens. I don't think I have been on a platform with as many men and women who have contributed so much to the cultural, recreational, and dynamic growth of America as are gathered here today. These are people who have creativity, who have the willingness to accept responsibility, who are willing to give of*

Saratoga Performing Arts Center, aerial view. *Photo provided by the Saratoga Performing Arts Center.*

> *their time in the service of the community, whether it's in education, arts, or various phases of cultural life or recreation.*[32]

George Balanchine believed in the positive effect the performing arts could have on the region. Barbara Horgan, his personal assistant, said, "Balanchine's intent was to bring our particular art form to the area, which he thought could and would have a renaissance."[33]

Both George Balanchine and Eugene Ormandy sat on the original board of directors of the Saratoga Performing Arts Center along with a who's who of Saratoga society, influential businessmen and New York State and civic leaders. The slate of officers of the board of directors included Mrs. Nelson Rockefeller, chairwoman; Gene Robb, president; Newman E. Wait Jr., treasurer; and Charles J. LaBelle, secretary.[34]

Lewis A. Swyer, owner of the construction company that built the facility and a great supporter of the arts, joined the board of directors in 1968. He then became president and chairman of the board, positions he held proudly from 1974 until his death in 1988.[35]

THE FESTIVAL OPENS AT THE SARATOGA PERFORMING ARTS CENTER

The New York City Ballet was now the first ballet company in the country to have a summer home, and what a home it was! The amphitheater had a seating capacity of 5,200 and the potential to accommodate thousands more on the lawn. The facility included spacious rehearsal studios and a stage with a state-of-the-art flooring system that was constructed for maximum resiliency. Without question, this would be the largest audience and the largest stage the New York City Ballet had ever experienced.

On July 8, 1966, at 8:30 p.m., the First Saratoga Festival opened with the New York City Ballet accompanied by its own orchestra in a performance of George Balanchine's *A Midsummer Night's Dream.* For four weeks, the local audience enjoyed one of the best ballet companies in the world as it performed ballets by one of the century's greatest choreographers.

Dancer Robert Maiorano remembers Balanchine's comment to the dancers prior to going to Saratoga for the first time: "We must educate the audience slowly, to bring them to us. That is what culture is for, to raise people up and bring them out of the doldrums."[36]

The company roster included some very famous principal dancers. Ballerinas Suzanne Farrell, Melissa Hayden and Patricia McBride each had her individual style. Edward Villella, Jacques D'Amboise and Arthur Mitchell were famous American dancers who had appeared in film and on television. Audiences chose their favorites and tried to spot young, upcoming talents in the corps de ballet. However, the biggest star of all was a man who did not perform onstage: George Balanchine.

Opening night of the New York City Ballet at the Saratoga Performing Arts Center. *Program provided by the Saratoga Performing Arts Center archives.*

Twenty-nine ballets were performed that first summer. Some entertained, while others challenged the audience. Most of the ballets were choreographed by George Balanchine or Jerome Robbins, the two ballet masters of the New York City Ballet. Other works by Anthony Tudor, Merce Cunningham, John Taras and Edward Villella were included in the company's diverse repertoire. Lincoln Kirstein explained one of Balanchine's theories that was evident to the audience in his choreography: "Balanchine knew that the twentieth century needed its own tempi, which were jazzy and syncopated, and that asymmetrical rhythm was deep in the motor dynamism of advanced industrial societies."[37]

Saratoga's audiences were treated to a great range of musical styles in the ballets performed during the first season. The excellent New York City Ballet Orchestra was led by musical director and principal conductor Robert Irving and by assistant conductor Hugo Fiorato. Maestro Irving had been conductor for Britain's Royal Ballet before he joined New York City Ballet. According to Lincoln Kirstein, Irving "eventually turned into a real New Yorker, and later in Saratoga, he was a passionate racer of horses!"[38]

NEW YORK CITY BALLET

FRIDAY, July 8, 1966 at 8:30 p.m.
(Benefit Previews for the Center's Educational Fund)
Conductor: Robert Irving

SATURDAY, July 9, 1966 at 8:30 p.m.
Conductor: Robert Irving

SUNDAY, July 10, 1966 at 8:30 p.m.
Conductor: Hugo Fiorato

A Midsummer Night's Dream

(Ballet in Two Acts and Six Scenes)

Music by Felix Mendelssohn (Overture and Incidental Music to *A Midsummer Night's Dream;* Overtures to: *Son and Stranger, Athalie, Fair Melusine;* Symphony for Strings, No. 9; *The First Walpurgis Night*)

Choreography by George Balanchine

Costumes by Karinska

Scenery and Lighting by David Hays

SINGERS

Mildred Fling, soprano   Batyah Godfrey, mezzo-soprano

and

Carol Cramer, Lois Crane, Esther Harmos, Joyce Hankerson, Frances Hoggard, Irene Kessler, Joyce Gerber, Susanah Martin, Jane Murray, Linda Phillips, Joy Ryan, Alice Shields

Début performance of New York City Ballet at the Saratoga Performing Arts Center. *Program provided by the Saratoga Performing Arts Center archives.*

A Midsummer Night's Dream, choreography by George Balanchine. ©The George Balanchine Trust, Arthur Mitchell and Suki Schorer with dancers. *Photo by Fred Fehl.*

The spontaneous relationship created among musicians, dancers and the audience was described by Kirstein: "Our audiences in New York and in Saratoga have, over the years, accustomed themselves to our insistence on making them listen hard at the same moments when they look with attention. A minimum of visual adornment and emphasis on unfamiliar rhythms and sonorities demand a concentration which is willing to accept a certain didactic tyranny."[39]

The ballets *Firebird*, *A Midsummer Night's Dream* and *Harlequinade* required the addition of young dancers to the cast. Many local ballet students auditioned for the opportunity to appear onstage with the company. These performances generated a surge in ticket sales as family and friends flocked to the Saratoga Performing Arts Center to see the young performers on stage.

In addition to performances by the New York City Ballet and by the Philadelphia Orchestra, the American Dressage Institute presented demonstrations of baroque equestrian art. Riders from the Viennese Spanish Riding School and their famous Lipizzaner stallions performed on the lawn in the evenings before the ballet. Balanchine himself learned to ride so he could participate in the beautiful ballet of horses that "danced" to the music of Handel, Hayden, Mozart and Lanner.[40] Mr. Balanchine later gave the dancers horse blankets to stay warm offstage in the wings on chilly evenings. He even had them embroidered with the dancers' names.[41]

NEW YORK CITY BALLET MAKES ITSELF AT HOME IN SARATOGA SPRINGS

This was the beginning of a love affair between Saratoga Springs and the dancers from the New York City Ballet. Many company dancers shared fond memories of the first season. Edward Villella, one of the company's biggest stars, recalled, "My first and lasting impressions are of the great outdoors, the beauty of the trees and grass and sunshine, light and air, a connection with nature."[42]

Soloist Robert Maiorano remembered, "All the dancers loved being in Saratoga right from the beginning. How lucky we were to be dancing in such a beautiful place that had been built for us! It was summertime outside; there were little boys running on the lawn and a cacophony of tree frogs

Principal dancer Suzanne Farrell at the Saratoga Race Course. *Photo provided by the New York City Ballet archives.*

and bugs all around you."[43] Melissa Hayden said, "We danced on that big stage in the fresh air with more abandon, more freedom; everyone danced from their hearts." Shaun O'Brien described a sense of family: "There was a special camaraderie. We were very close that first summer because it was a new experience, and Mr. B. was so pleased it was working out; he was a little closer to us."[44]

Andrew Wentink, author, archivist and a former dancer, explained, "Balanchine embraced America, and to him, Saratoga represented America. His enjoyment gave his dancers permission to enjoy it all themselves, to respond and become a part of it all." Wentink went regularly to see the company perform in New York. He marveled at the effect that the Saratoga experience had on the dancers: "Seeing the performances outdoors on a beautiful summer night was magical. All the dancers were much more relaxed here in Saratoga. Their dancing was different—transformed somehow. They were really dancing for the local audience, knowing the audience loved having them here."[45]

That first summer, the dancers stayed a bit out of town at the Ashgrove Inn. Maiorano explained, "We were New Yorkers, and nobody drove in those days. We were bussed in and out, and we walked up and down on Broadway. People saw us and stopped to talk; they were thrilled that we were here. I recall there were only a few restaurants downtown back then—D'Andrea's, The Executive on Phila Street and especially Hatties on the west side of town that stayed open late, even after the late-night poker games!"

Both Balanchine and Robbins had hoped to use time in Saratoga for creative work, away from the urban pressures of New York City. However, "it soon became clear that there would be little time available for preparation of new ballets. Current repertoire was maintained with efficiency, but swimming pools, horse racing, and Lake George were relaxations too powerful to resist. The dancers needed rest. In the exuberance of enjoyment, there were hazards—broken toes from soccer games played recklessly in bare feet, ferocious sunburn, and too much dosing with mineral water."[46]

They rehearsed, performed and relaxed right there in the park. A favorite destination of all the dancers was the Victoria Pool, where they could rest in the sun and soak their tired legs and feet in the cool water. Peter Martins said, "I always loved summers in Saratoga, and my favorite part was the Victoria Pool, where I lived when I wasn't dancing."[47] Some dancers even cast fishing lines from the surrounding boulders into the creek near the amphitheater. This certainly was not the way they relaxed between rehearsals at Lincoln Center!

After a few seasons, dancers began renting houses or apartments for the month in Saratoga Springs. Some had learned to drive especially for the summers in Saratoga, and they rented cars from Rent-a-Wreck. Dancers

Dancers fishing off the boulders in Spa State Park during rehearsal break. *Photo provided by the New York City Ballet archives.*

were now able to enjoy outings on Saratoga Lake, swim at the quarry or explore the Adirondacks on days off.

The New York City Ballet was becoming a real part of the community during the summer. Locals frequently ran into dancers in grocery stores

George Balanchine and Eddie Bigelow at River Run Farm. *Photo provided by Mrs. Kay Leach. BALANCHINE is a trademark of The George Balanchine Trust.*

or at gas stations, and folks knew many dancers by first name. Some of the company members stayed downtown at the Adelphi Hotel, and others stayed on the Skidmore College campus in the Scribner Village apartments.

Many dancers bought vacation homes in Saratoga. Michael Steele was the first in 1968, and he encouraged his friends to follow. Dancers Shaun O'Brien, Robert Maiorano, Anthony Blum, Leslie Roy and David Otto and musicians LaMar and Ruth Alsop all settled here permanently.[48]

Every July, George Balanchine stayed in a guest cottage at River Run Farm, the rural property of Richard and Kay Leach. Eddie Bigelow, production manager of the company, took the second-floor apartment. Balanchine was passionate about cooking, and he loved to garden. His dancers say he often used cooking imagery to describe what he wanted in the studio. Kay Leach explained:

> *I tried to prepare everything he might need. We planted a special garden for George with herbs like coriander and sorrel. In the mornings, he sat outside on the patio in his wrap, drinking café au lait and enjoying pastries from Mrs. London's. One of my dogs loved George and insisted on staying in the cottage with him. We had heaps of dogs and heaps of cats, heaps of goats,*

> *horses, and donkeys. July was the happiest time—like a dream; it was such a wonderful period in our lives.*[49]

Mrs. Leach often carried bundles of Mrs. London's pastries when she visited Mr. B. in New York. "He says he doesn't want to talk ballet, and that all he dreams about from July to July are these confections!"[50]

THE NEXT DECADE—THE BALLET BOOM OF THE 1970S

The decade of the 1970s was a high time for ballet across the country. In Saratoga Springs, New York City Ballet audiences enjoyed several noteworthy "firsts." The Saratoga Performing Arts Center commissioned two new ballets for the Saratoga season. The full-length ballet *Coppélia*, featuring principal dancers Patricia McBride and Helgi Tomasson, had its world premier in Saratoga in 1974. This charming nineteenth-century French ballet was staged by George Balanchine and Alexandra Danilova. Mme. Danilova was a famous ballerina with Ballet Russe de Monte Carlo and a beloved teacher at the School of American Ballet. The second commissioned ballet, Balanchine's *The Steadfast Tin Soldier*, had its world premier in July 1975. Based on a tale by Hans Christian Anderson, this ballet also starred Patricia McBride, with guest principal dancer from Denmark Peter Schaufuss.

The company continued to bring repertoire from its Lincoln Center seasons to premier in Saratoga. The New York City Ballet broke all box office records when it brought George Balanchine's *Nutcracker* to Saratoga in July 1972. This holiday ballet was performed for an audience of more than six thousand people.[51] Ballet master Jerome Robbins premiered his ballet *Goldberg Variations* in Saratoga in 1971. Robbins's *Dances at a Gathering* was especially successful in the open-air setting, which enhanced the ballet's atmosphere with breezes and fireflies on the lawn.[52] New works by principal dancer Peter Martins were introduced, foreshadowing his future as a prolific choreographer for the company.

Cris Alexander, Steven Caras and Paul Kolnik are among the many photographers who specialized in photographing the dancers of the New York City Ballet. Kolnick has been taking photos of the New York City Ballet since the 1970s and is still the official photographer for the company. Kolnick said:

Coppélia, Act III, choreography by George Balanchine and Alexandra Danilova. ©The George Balanchine Trust, Patricia McBride, Helgi Tomasson and dancers. *Photo by Martha Swope.*

> *Balanchine changed my life. He happened to use the language of ballet, a clear and articulate language. Now, all I want to do is illuminate Balanchine's work. I like photographing in Saratoga, because different things happen here. At SPAC, with the sound of the little stream, the birds, the smell of the pines, there's an added dimension that fills up the senses. The ballets seem to expand here. Half of my best pictures are taken here, though I only spend one-eighth of my time here. Saratoga is ballet heaven for me.*[53]

Saratoga dance fans were thrilled to learn that world-famous dancer Mikhail Baryshnikov would be performing with the New York City Ballet during the summer of 1979. Peter Martins remembers, "In recalling times in Saratoga, I particularly enjoyed when Misha was there, performing with us. Misha had so many fans that he had to escape via the orchestra lounge back door, so he wouldn't be swamped by autograph seekers. There would be a car waiting for him, and I always enjoyed the ride up the hill (not that anyone was looking for *my* autograph!)."[54]

The local audience saw familiar dancers retire and new artists emerge. Many who were in the corps de ballet in 1966 were now soloists, including Shaun O'Brien, Robert Weiss and Robert Maiorano. Some soloists from the 1960s had become principal dancers, such as Kay Mazzo, Sara Leland and Carol Sumner. The company itself had grown tremendously. Back in 1966, the New York City Ballet was an ensemble of 56 dancers; by 1980, the roster had increased to 101.

George Balanchine and Jerome Robbins share a light moment in rehearsal. *Photo from the collection of the National Museum of Dance. BALANCHINE is a trademark of The George Balanchine Trust.*

Public relations icon Ed Lewi began working for the Saratoga Performing Arts Center in 1969. He says, "I was conscripted to work for SPAC by the first president, Gene Robb. I was a sports nut who didn't know anything about ballet. In the beginning I worked for free with a paid assistant. For the first time in my career, I didn't know my topic—I had to investigate and learn more about SPAC and this New York City Ballet."

Ed Lewi tried some creative ideas to identify the New York City Ballet specifically with life in Saratoga Springs. To the delight of the local audience,

George Balanchine coaches Mikhail Baryshnikov in *Orpheus*, choreography by George Balanchine. *©The George Balanchine Trust. Photo from the collection of the National Museum of Dance. BALANCHINE is a trademark of The George Balanchine Trust.*

Lewi convinced a well-known local banker to participate in a performance of the ballet *Slaughter on Tenth Ave.* He photographed ballerinas with Thoroughbreds and brought Edward Villella to speak at local Rotary and Kiwanis Club meetings. Ed Lewi organized groups of ballet dancers and musicians to perform at a prison near Plattsburg.

In the effort to increase attendance, Lewi initiated the "Theme Nights," which proved to be very popular. The programming for each evening followed a particular theme, such as American Composers Night, All-Russian Night or All-Stravinsky Night.

Ed Lewi told the story of his first experience with George Balanchine:

> *Balanchine came to me early on and said, "Lewi, I hear you don't like the ballet." He gave me a list of ballets he wanted me to see—the lighter ones so I would learn to like it. Those that weren't on the list, Balanchine told me to stay in my office. It worked—I learned a lot about the ballets, the*

> *dancers and the audience. I even got on stage! One night Balanchine told me, "Lewi, you're going to be in Firebird tonight." Like hell I am! There I was, a super on stage* in tights *in the final scene.*

"Not a highlight of my life," he added with a grin. Even after his retirement, Ed Lewi has remained with the Saratoga Performing Arts Center, serving as the secretary of the board of directors.[55]

Dancers had several favorite destinations for relaxing after performances. Sperry's and Hattie's were popular, and those former dancers who now lived in Saratoga frequently hosted their friends. The primary nightspot was the garden lounge at the Adelphi Hotel, where dancers mingled with local fans. The ballet orchestra members often played chamber music in the hotel ballroom, creating a scene reminiscent of Saratoga's gilded age.

Sheila Parkert was the owner of the Adelphi at that time, and she remembered those evenings fondly:

> *The relationship between Saratoga Springs and the company was very friendly and warm—like family. They loved us and we loved them. Mr. Balanchine loved all his dancers, current and past, and he always welcomed them to him. We took it all in stride; I guess we didn't realize history was being made.*[56]

Former dancer with the company and musician Daniel Duell said:

> *I recall very elegant evenings of chamber music supplied by the NYCB Orchestra members in the ballroom of the hotel. The décor was classic, dark wood furnishings, highly polished, very tasty cuisine and generous drinks. Robert Irving conducted in 1986–87, the two years I participated as flutist. The chamber orchestra played Tchaikovsky, Bach, Handel and other composers. Those evenings brought musicians and listeners close, as much NYCB repertoire was played. We could just play the music already dear to the audience's hearts from having seen the ballets. It was joy, joy, joy. The warmth of the audience response and the dancers also coming in to listen because they too so loved just hearing the music they danced to—all this because Mr. B. brought us all so close to music through his ballets.*[57]

Andrew Wentink stated, "George Balanchine was there frequently—he was present. Talk about a heady environment! Saratoga Springs now knew the social *and* artistic elite of the times."[58]

For over a century, Saratoga Springs has been known for parties in the summer. Many prominent local people wanted to celebrate the dancers. The Wait family held an annual private party at their Lake George property. Mrs. Ogden Phipps entertained the dancers with a pool party every summer.

Although Mr. Balanchine did not frequent the social scene, he did arrange a great party at his River Run cottage for Mikhail Baryshnikov. According to Kay Leach, Balanchine dictated the menu, including blini and four pounds of caviar brought up to Saratoga from Zabar's in New York City. Balanchine himself entertained at the piano, impersonating many celebrities. Mrs. Leach told a story of one of the farm animals: "One of our goats on the farm could jump very high—high enough to get on top of the shed. We named him Misha in honor of Baryshnikov's great leaps."[59]

As hard as dancers work, they must also have time to play. Kathryn Levy, from the New York City Ballet Education Department, remembers an amusing tradition that took place in Saratoga:

> *New York choreographer Peter Anastos used to stage parody ballets in a parking lot in Saratoga. Everyone in the company would come. One time, he staged a parody of Robbins's* Glass Pieces *called "Price Chopper Variations." It involved people running across the "stage" very rapidly to Philip Glass music, pushing big shopping carts à la Price Chopper. It was a big hit!*[60]

SARATOGA SPRINGS CELEBRATES GEORGE BALANCHINE

The community of Saratoga Springs looked forward to the annual return of the New York City Ballet. Every July, downtown store windows posted signs welcoming the company back, and banners hung across Broadway. Mayor Raymond Watkin exclaimed:

> *When the New York City Ballet is in town, it changes the character of the city for the better. It is an exciting time that gives the people a good lift. This is a very fine thing that happens here in Saratoga Springs.*

In the summer of 1977, Mayor Raymond Watkin declared Friday, July 15, to be George Balanchine Day, and Saratoga Springs celebrated with a grand parade down Broadway. Mr. Balanchine and Mayor Watkin rode together in a

George Balanchine Day. Mr. Balanchine with Mayor Raymond Watkin and Michael Arshansky enjoying the festivities. *Photo provided by Mayor Watkin. BALANCHINE is a trademark of The George Balanchine Trust.*

horse-drawn antique surrey. New York City Ballet dancers, dressed appropriately in the costumes from *Stars and Stripes*, rode a decorated fire truck. Groups of local dancers, drum majorettes and bands marched through the center of town as hundreds of people cheered for "Mr. B" when he passed by. Governor Hugh Carey sat in the viewing stand along with Balanchine's close friend Michael Arshansky, who was in costume as the mayor from *Coppélia*.[61]

After laudatory speeches, Mayor Watkin presented George Balanchine with the Keys to the City. Balanchine spoke from the podium:

> *I don't know where I can enter with this key, but I will find a place. When they accept things like this in Hollywood they say they couldn't have done it without so and so. I must say we couldn't have done it without the bodies, and so I will share this key with all my girls. We love to go here, and I wish we could stay longer.*[62]

On stage before the performance that evening, Mayor Watkin handed Balanchine a commemorative plaque. The proclamation read:

Mayor Raymond Watkin presents George Balanchine with the Keys to the City. *Photo provided by Mayor Watkin. BALANCHINE is a trademark of The George Balanchine Trust.*

> *The New York City Ballet, under the guidance of Mr. Balanchine, has had immeasurable impact upon our community in terms of both culture and economics. Dance has become a way of life in Saratoga, and people are drawn from miles around to view this remarkable company on our stage. Numerous schools of ballet have come into being in the area because of the interest in dance generated by the New York City Ballet. Saratoga Springs salutes George Balanchine, one of Saratoga's most distinguished citizens.*[63]

Mr. Balanchine, who usually preferred to remain in the background, was pleased with it all.

Mayor Watkin still has great regard for Balanchine and an appreciation for the impact the company has had on the community. "He was such an interesting guy. Balanchine was a very talented fellow. He wanted perfection; he brought in new things, introducing us to music and his style of dance. Balanchine educated us about Stravinsky. A lot of people didn't like it, but he really wanted to educate his public. I liked it."[64]

Ironically, even after eleven summers of beautiful performances and that summer's citywide celebrations, in 1977 the New York City Ballet and Saratoga Performing Arts Center made the joint decision to shorten the ballet season to three weeks.

The Saratoga Performing Arts Center's directors had implemented popular programming that generated revenue, but the shortfall from ticket sales and overall costs of the ballet season were growing year by year. The situation was exacerbated by an unexpected cutback in funding from the state. Herb Chesbrough, the executive director at that time, stated clearly, "Unless SPAC can get the additional $125,000 in funding it figured on from the New York Council on the Arts when it planned for the full ballet season, it simply cannot afford the fourth week."[65]

Led by Mayor Watkin, concerned local citizens and many determined fans advocated strenuously against the cutback. Mayor Watkin convinced the Saratoga Springs City Council to give $25,000 to the Saratoga Performing Arts Center. He wrote a letter in protest directly to Governor Hugh Carey and distributed it to other state officials. Mayor Watkin went to Albany to testify about the benefits the New York City Ballet brought to his city: "This was really important, not only culturally but economically that the ballet be here. I worked very hard for this; I fought for what I believed in!"[66]

The End of an Era and the Beginning of Another

The 1980s brought huge changes to the New York City Ballet. Mr. Balanchine was ill, and principal dancer and choreographer Peter Martins was being groomed to take over the company:

IN MEMORIAM

GEORGE BALANCHINE

The members of the Board of Directors of the Saratoga Performing Arts Center deeply mourn the passing of George Balanchine.

Mr. Balanchine and the New York City Ballet were one of the cornerstones in the birth and growth of the Saratoga Performing Arts Center. The beauty and inspiration of Mr. Balanchine's work has changed the heart and soul of this community to the appreciation of music and the dance. His name is inscribed in the hearts of us who have been the beneficiaries of his creative genius.

The Saratoga Performing Arts Center gave Mr. Balanchine his largest audiences. They continue as a memorial to him.

The Saratoga Performing Arts Center

Memorial to George Balanchine, Saratoga Performing Arts Center program. *BALANCHINE is a trademark of The George Balanchine Trust.*

It was at SPAC in the mid-'70s that Martins first got word from Balanchine that he was a likely heir to the ageing master's throne. "I remember getting a call from Balanchine one morning. I was living in the dorms at Skidmore. The phone rang, and he said, 'Come for lunch at Sperry's.'" Martins recalled. "He said to me out of the blue, 'You see, dear, you'll have to run this place, New York City Ballet. One day you'll have to run the company, and so we have to begin to teach you.' He didn't ask me, he told me. He took me by surprise."[67]

After several years of deteriorating health, George Balanchine died in 1983. He left a legacy of masterworks and the great company he had created. Peter Martins retired from performing and joined Jerome Robbins as co–ballet masters in chief. That decade at the Saratoga Performing Arts Center, the programs featured ballets by Martins and Robbins, although the foundation of the repertoire was still the collection of George Balanchine's ballets.

During the summer of 1985, the New York City Ballet celebrated its twentieth anniversary of performing in Saratoga with a whole week of *A Midsummer Night's Dream*, the ballet that started it all. Ballet fans were discovering new favorites as the New York City Ballet found its new identity. Saratoga audiences said goodbye to their favorite ballerina, Patricia McBride, when she retired from the stage after her final performance at the 1989 Ballet Gala. Future stars Darci Kistler, Jock Soto, Wendy Whelan and Damian Woetzel were all in the corps de ballet in the early 1980s and quickly rose to principal status.

Peter Martins explained:

First of all, as I grew older and into my non-dancing phase, each year I became more appreciative of SPAC and its importance in the life of New York City Ballet. I essentially continued Balanchine's maxim, which was that Saratoga deserves exactly what our New York audiences get to see. So I try every year to do just that, however in a minimized version.[68]

The 1990 season marked twenty-five years of the New York City Ballet in Saratoga. To celebrate, the company performed a retrospective selection of ballets that represented each of the past twenty-four seasons. During this decade, Peter Martins debuted his staging of two full-length classic ballets: *Sleeping Beauty* and *Swan Lake*. These were large productions, and both ballets were great favorites of the audience. To commemorate the tenth anniversary

Jerome Robbins, choreographer and co–ballet master in chief. *Photo by Ohringer.*

of Balanchine's death, the company paid tribute by performing twenty-four of his ballets in one season. Jerome Robbins assembled dance scenes from his famous Broadway musical *West Side Story* into a suite that was very popular with Saratoga audiences.

Ballet master in chief Peter Martins considers the pursuit of new works to be "the life blood of the company."[69] Martins initiated the Diamond Project in 1992. This sponsored program enabled him to commission choreographers such as Alexei Ratmansky and Christopher Wheeldon and to introduce them to the Saratoga audience. The Diamond Project has continued since then, enabling dozens of choreographers to create work for the company dancers.

Unfortunately, attendance at the ballet continued to decline. Although the season remained at three weeks, the Saratoga Performing Arts Center reduced the total number of ballet performances and presented more popular entertainment.

The Twenty-First Century

To encourage audiences of all ages, the Saratoga Performing Arts Center, New York City Ballet and several sponsors scheduled promotional theme nights. These events often included pre-curtain activities. Ballets were chosen to appeal to specific audiences, such as young dance students and their parents, young adults or families. The success of these sponsored theme nights has made them annual events: Junior Ballerina Night, Girls' Night Out, Sage Colleges Date Night, CDPHP Family Night and Emma Willard American Girl Night.

The tenth anniversary of the Diamond Project was celebrated in 2002 with a variety of new works offered at the Saratoga Performing Arts Center. Christopher Wheeldon was named the New York City Ballet's first choreographer in residence. Wheeldon's light-hearted *Carnival of the Animals*, featuring the comedian and actor John Lithgow, was a big success with Saratoga audiences. Local writer Mae Banner said of the ballet, "Lithgow wrote and narrated the rhyming libretto…and also did a dainty turn as a humongous lady elephant in this whimsical confection. Wheeldon and Lithgow set out a plateful of sweets in this fantasy about a child locked in overnight at the Museum of Natural History."[70]

In another of her reviews for the *Saratogian*, Ms. Banner wrote:

> *Symphony in Three Movements is one of the great collaborations between Stravinsky and Balanchine, and it has never looked better. The dancers out-did themselves, thrilling the audience from the first moment of this well-wrought leotard ballet. Wendy Whelan and Jock Soto in the central duet were like lifelong lovers who finished each other's sentences. The air between them zinged and crackled. One would query with the gesture of a leg; the other would answer with a leg. The amphitheater erupted in prolonged applause at the finale of this knife-edged dance…Saratoga audiences do know a good thing when they see it.*[71]

For more than forty years, Saratoga audiences have witnessed final performances of many of their favorite dancers as they retired from the stage. In July 2004, Jock Soto was celebrated by hundreds of his fans. Mae Banner described the homage to one of her personal favorites: "The luckiest and most fervent NYCB fans come every night to see something unexpected and wonderful. At the July 17 Gala, Jock Soto was showered with flowers after dancing his last performance in Saratoga, a sculpted 'Barber Violin Concerto'…a loving audience gave him an emotional sendoff."[72]

The fortieth-anniversary season began once again with *A Midsummer Night's Dream.* Popular ballets by Balanchine and Robbins and new works by Martins and Wheeldon formed the bulk of the repertoire. Other highlights were Jerome Robbins's *NY Export: Opus Jazz,* a new work by Alexiei Ratmansky from the Diamond Project and a premier by former principal dancer Benjamin Millepied.

Peter Martins's full-length ballet *Romeo+Juliet* introduced a cast of very young dancers in the principal roles. This production drew in large audiences who loved the familiar story and Prokofiev's music.

In his review of *The Waltz Project*, local dance critic Jay Rogoff stated:

> *Peter Martins' lively ballet characterizes four couples in piano waltzes by nine contemporary American composers. Originally scheduled for SPAC in 1988,* The Waltz Project *was scratched that summer because of a string of injuries. Thursday's performance, with a cast entirely new to the ballet, revealed it as charming, intriguing, and a little scary. Its format, a series of brief duets, makes it a distant cousin of Jerome Robbins'* In the Night, *also showing this season. Martins paints his characters less richly and subtly than Robbins, but his waltzers' relationships offer greater variety, with two compatible couples and two problematic ones.*[73]

A summer 2012 review in the *New York Times* stated:

> *It's startling how different NYCB looks at the open-air SPAC. The light has the effect of subtly changing faces, feet, musculature. Choreography, too. As I watched two performances here on Saturday, works as familiar as George Balanchine's "Concerto Barocco" and "Symphony in C" suddenly revealed fresh details. The dancers looked happy, despite the afternoon heat, as if performing for friends. A high quotient of young people in the audience cheered and clapped at every opportunity.*[74]

SARATOGA PERFORMING ARTS CENTER ADMINISTRATIVE DECISIONS

The Saratoga Performing Arts Center made major changes in its administration in 2005. In the same year as the fortieth anniversary of the Arts Center, Marcia White became the new president and executive director. Ms. White organized a new board of directors with William Dake, chairman, and the return of Mrs. Marylou Whitney, honorary chairwoman. Several local arts personalities and businessmen have since been added to the board, such as Dolores "Dee" Sarno, Skidmore's Donald McCormack, Heather Mabee, Ronald Riggi and current chairwoman Susan Phillips Read.

Due to mounting financial losses on both sides, in 2009 the New York City Ballet and Saratoga Performing Arts Center made a second joint decision to reduce the ballet season from three to two weeks. The Saratoga Springs community rallied in protest, but the realities of production costs, low attendance numbers and poor ticket revenues could not be argued.

After the 2012 season, it was announced that the New York City Ballet would come to Saratoga in 2013 for only one week. Two other dance companies would complete the remainder of the classical dance programming—the National Ballet of Canada and a contemporary American company, the Aspen/Santa Fe Ballet.[75]

Marcia White shared her thoughts on the relationship among the Saratoga Performing Arts Center, the New York City Ballet and Saratoga Springs:

> *SPAC has always been something incredibly important to my whole family. My daughters and I grew up on this lawn together, and one of them performed in* Coppélia *for four summers. I had great educational opportunities and a background that gave me diverse skills from marketing to politics to triage. When I came to this position, we all embraced change, and we made change to regain the public trust. SPAC has a legacy and a heritage established over time. We have two magnificent resident companies, and they are our backbone. However, these times are different from earlier days, and we must deal with the realities of the situation as it is now. Together, we—NYCB and SPAC—must establish something that is sustainable and as close as possible to the "glory days" that the fans yearn for. The quality of life in the Saratoga area is greatly enhanced by the arts. SPAC has helped to generate many millions of dollars into the local economy, and the arts have helped to attract major corporations and businesses to the area. I'm very proud of that. I'm also proud of SPAC's educational programs; we really want that next generation of artists and audiences to be here! The arts lift us up in hard times, and the "SPAC Experience"—seeing great art on a beautiful summer evening in a beautiful outdoor setting—provides that lift.*[76]

OTHER DANCE EVENTS AT THE SARATOGA PERFORMING ARTS CENTER

In addition to the New York City Ballet, there have been several other dance companies and dance events featured at the Saratoga Performing Arts Center. In 1967, the Russian Music and Dance Festival included the Ukranian Dance Company, Oldavian Dancers, Uzbek Dancers and several soloists from Moscow's famous Bolshoi Ballet. The great ballerina Margot Fonteyn of Britain's Royal Ballet appeared in 1975 with the Chicago Ballet. During the 1990s, the Miami City Ballet, led by former New York City Ballet star Edward Villella, and the Irish dance and music phenomenon *Riverdance* appeared. These two companies were so popular that they were brought back the following season.

Dancers have also performed with the Philadelphia Orchestra during their August seasons. *Rudolf Nureyev and Friends* appeared during the summer of 1986. New York City Ballet principal dancers Merrill Ashley and John Meehan performed with the Philadelphia Orchestra, led by New York City Ballet conductor Robert Irving.[77] For the final classical performance of 2012, dancers Tiler Peck and Chase Finlay performed the Act II pas de deux from *Swan Lake* during the Philadelphia Orchestra's Tchaikovsky Spectacular.

A unique cultural dance event was held on the lawn in 2012. The Saratoga Native American Festival featured the Haudenosaunee Singers and Dancers, a popular performing troupe from Syracuse. This festival was sponsored by the Ndakinna Education Center and the Spa State Park.[78]

The Saratoga Performing Arts Center Walk of Fame, located on the mezzanine pavement before entering the amphitheater, was established at the Saratoga Performing Arts Center in 2010. To date, three honorees have been recognized with an engraved bronze star inset into the flooring. Mrs. Marylou Whitney was the first to be honored for her many years of personal and financial commitment to dance in Saratoga Springs. The following year, George Wein, jazz impresario and founder of the Freihofer's Saratoga Jazz Festival, was inducted. In 2012, Lewis A. Swyer, long-serving chairman and president of the Saratoga Performing Arts Center, was recognized for his vision and dedication to dance and the arts.[79]

Chapter 4
Dance Teachers and Dance Schools in Saratoga Springs

Many dancers train here; many dancers are inspired here. Saratoga Springs is well known as a "Dance Town."

Saratoga Springs is a small city with approximately twenty-eight thousand year-round residents. One attribute that makes Saratoga unique among cities of this size is the presence of dance in the community. Saratoga Springs currently has ten independent dance schools and a history of many more. Instruction ranges from the elegance of classical ballet to the exuberance of Latin salsa. These schools continue to thrive, occasionally changing location to accommodate a growing enrollment. The local dance studios help to build a knowledgeable audience in a city that values the art of dance.

Prestigious dance schools and companies frequently hold auditions in Saratoga Springs. Hundreds of young dancers and their parents come to town to audition for the New York City Ballet, the New York State Summer School of the Arts Schools of Ballet and Dance and for many national summer intensive dance programs.

Saratoga Springs Dance Schools, 1900 to 1965

For two centuries, Saratoga Springs has had a dual personality as a small town for most of the year and a famous resort for the summer. The local population has developed a higher cultural awareness than that of many other small towns because of this exposure. Dance, and dancing, was an important part of the cultural and social fabric. Those who teach dance have been employed in Saratoga since the time of the great hotels of the nineteenth century.

At the turn of the twentieth century, Miss Ryan's Saratoga Dancing Academy offered dance instruction to young ladies and gentlemen.[80] Several short-lived dance schools opened in the community from the 1930s to the 1950s. The students of the De Marco House of Dance performed in the newly built Spa Little Theatre. Jane and Gloria Conway, who owned a studio in Latham, opened the Conway Sisters Dance Studio in Saratoga in the 1950s. They taught jazz, tap and ballet, and their students performed annually in the Saratoga High School. The Dunster family of Ballston Spa held dance classes in Saratoga for a brief time after the Conway sisters closed their school.[81]

As a young girl, Peggy Delay was a student of the Conway Sisters and performed in local vaudeville shows at the Congress Theater. In 1959, she opened Stepping Star Dance and Gymnastics, the first full-time commercial dance school in Saratoga Springs. Ms. Delay's daughter excelled in gymnastics, and the school gradually changed its focus to recreational and competitive team gymnastics. Currently three generations of Delay women along with many other instructors teach in Stepping Star's custom studio space in Congress Plaza. Although she is now retired, Peggy Delay still teaches one class for "little ones" and oversees her school's annual dance recitals that showcase over four hundred students.[82]

Oleg Briansky, a former premier danseur from Europe was the first to introduce classical ballet to Saratoga Springs. Briansky drove through Saratoga in 1964, on his way to Montreal for a performance with ballerina Marina Svetlova.[83] He was suffering from career-ending arthritis and decided to stop in Saratoga to try the spa treatment. Briansky immediately decided that Saratoga would be an excellent location to realize his dream of a ballet academy for serious students who wanted to continue studying during the summer months.

Briansky approached Skidmore College and was given studio space and housing on the college's downtown campus. The Briansky Saratoga Ballet Center opened in July 1965, one year before the Saratoga Performing Arts Center. Briansky's school boasted a staff of excellent teachers. Co-director Mireille Briane and Michel Renault were from the Paris Opera Ballet. Joysanne Sidimus was a respected teacher from the National Ballet of Canada. Other well-known modern dance and ethnic dance teachers

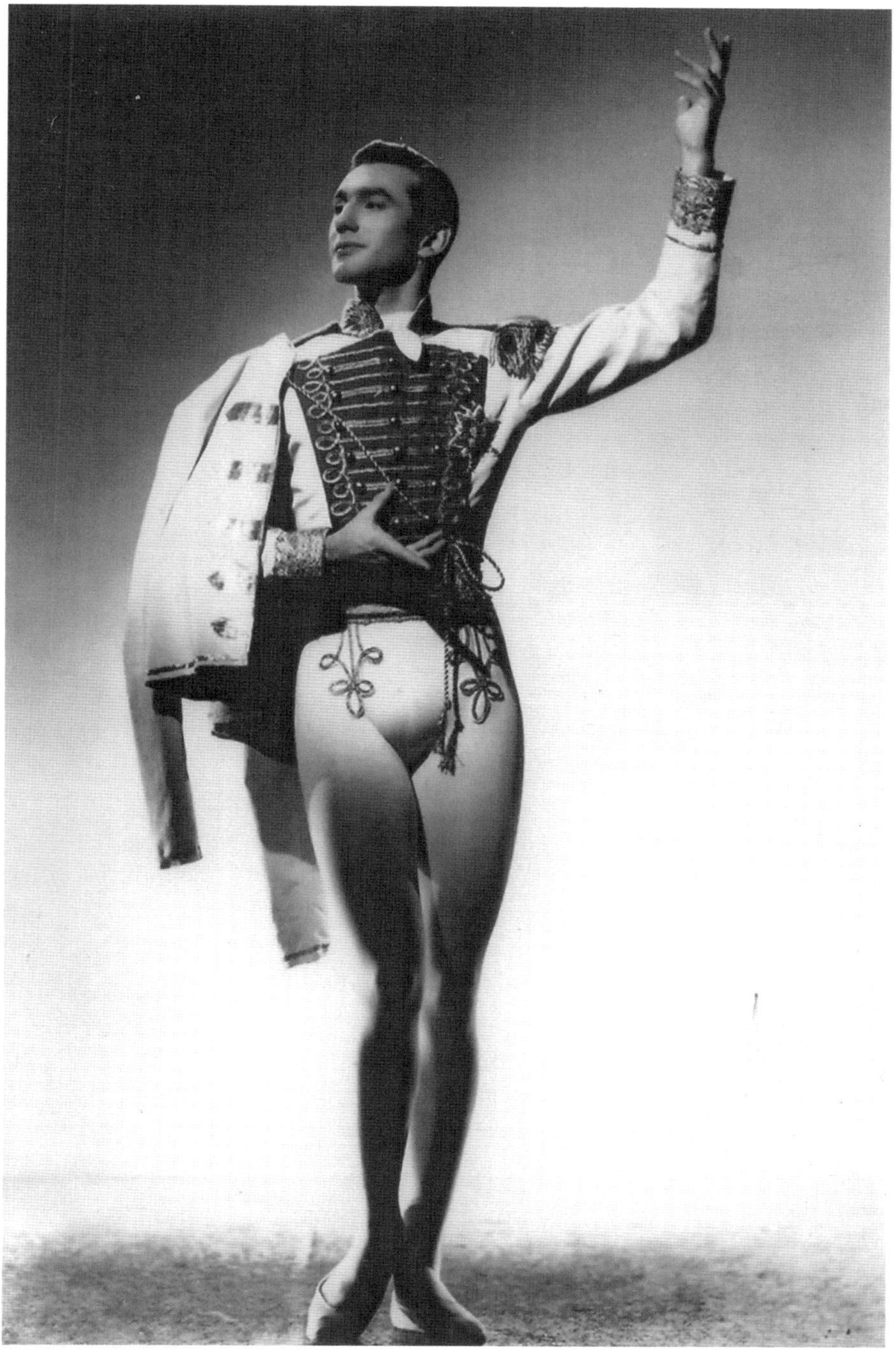

Oleg Briansky, premier danseur, owner of Briansky Saratoga Ballet Center. *Photo provided by Mr. Briansky.*

completed the faculty. After retiring from the New York City Ballet, Robert Maiorano taught regularly for Briansky, and before she joined Skidmore College, Debra Fernandez taught jazz for Briansky's program. The summer students attended New York City Ballet performances at the Saratoga Performing Arts Center, and many company dancers and staff taught master classes for the school. At a time when the New York City Ballet had just begun inspiring audiences with world-class performances, the Briansky Saratoga Ballet Center was offering a glimpse into the rigorous training necessary to develop young students into ballet dancers.

The Briansky Saratoga Ballet Center continued at Skidmore until 2008 and then relocated to the campus of Mount Holyoke College in western Massachusetts. Oleg Briansky and Mireille Briane declared, "We were pioneers. Who would ever guess, in such a small town one hundred seventy-five miles north of New York City, we would be a catalyst to help shape the artistic future of the city."[84]

The Influence of Skidmore College and the Saratoga Performing Arts Center on Local Schools

After just two seasons of performing at the Saratoga Performing Arts Center with the New York City Ballet, ballerina Melissa Hayden bought a home in Saratoga. She joined the Skidmore College dance faculty in 1974 and established her studio in the old Saratoga National Bank building on the corner of Broadway and Phila Street. In addition to teaching Skidmore's ballet dancers, Ms. Hayden developed a BOCES program for the Saratoga Springs City School District's talented children. She also held an intensive summer ballet program for students from around the region.

Melissa Hayden left Saratoga Springs in 1976 and was succeeded at Skidmore College by well-known ballerina Elisabeth Carroll. Like Ms. Hayden before her, Ms. Carroll and her husband, Felix Smith, were interested in teaching ballet to local children. They co-directed the Saratoga Dance Academy, a children's ballet school held in the campus studios. This community school was short lived, however, due to the increased demands placed on them by Skidmore's growing dance program.

A second ballet dancer, Phyllis Latin, moved to Saratoga in 1968 and began a ballet school in her large home on Union Avenue. Ms. Latin's performing career had been cut short by an automobile accident, so she began teaching dance. After moving the school to several locations, Phyllis Latin's American Dance Center secured a large space on the third floor of the Saratoga National Bank building. She taught in this studio for over thirty years.

Phyllis Latin founded the Saratoga Civic Ballet Company in 1971 with financial support from the CETA program.[85] She hired twelve dancers, many of whom lived in Ms. Latin's home, and a small staff. The company presented educational programs for schoolchildren and toured in the region. Michael Steele, former dancer with the New York City Ballet, worked for Ms. Latin as ballet master, and Patti Pugh, a student of both Briansky and Ms. Latin, performed with the company. With support of a wealthy patron, the Saratoga Civic Ballet Company traveled to Moscow, where it performed with Russian dancers.

After the first company closed, Phyllis Latin began the Phyllis Latin Dance Company in 2000. For several seasons, this company performed various styles of dance that appealed to a wide audience.

The American Dance Center still holds classes in the Swyer Studios of the National Museum of Dance. For over forty-four years, Phyllis Latin has taught hundreds of students who are now scattered throughout the dance world. She travels internationally to teach master classes in their schools, proudly promoting her former students and their many achievements. Phyllis Latin says, "I am old school, but I can't imagine dance without me or me without dance!"[86]

In 1968, Michael Steele was the first New York City Ballet dancer to buy a house in Saratoga Springs. He later left New York to perform in Europe, where he met dancer Tomislav Vukovic. They returned to Saratoga in 1978 to begin their professional ballet school, Ballet Regent. At the time, Michael Steele was quoted as saying, "I just wanted to get back to my beautiful little town in the country and teach ballet."[87] Steele had hoped to create a performing arts center in the old Regent Street Theater, but the plans for the building did not materialize. Ballet Regent moved to a space on Woodlawn Avenue before ultimately purchasing an old factory building on Jumel Place.

Steele and Vukovic were a complementary team in the studio. Steele taught the Balanchine style of precise movement and speed, and Vukovic, a former premier danseur from Yugoslavia, taught a more refined European classic style. Along the wall in the main studio at Ballet Regent is one of Michael Steele's favorite quotes by Lincoln Kirstein: "Ballet is about how to behave."

Michael Steele, owner of Ballet Regent. *Photo provided by Hattie's Restaurant.*

The Ballet Regent Summer Institute attracted students from all over the country. New York City Ballet dancers and Skidmore dance faculty taught frequently for both the summer and year-round sessions.

Most ballet schools struggle with a lack of male dancers. Michael Steele's particularly inspired solution to this challenge was his class "Pas de Dads," a pas de deux class for his most advanced girls and their fathers. The young ballerinas and their cavaliers learned partnering techniques and choreography. The Pas de Dads couples performed with great success in the spring performances.

Michael Steele died in his home in 2011. Tomi Vukovic moved to Florida, where he teaches ballet. They have left a legacy of many beautifully trained ballet dancers. The Ballet Regent studios are still in use and currently house several dance schools.[88]

In 1980, another commercial dance school, the Dance Factory, began offering classes in tap, jazz, ballet, lyrical and hip-hop. Director Dianne Carola was the primary dance teacher and an experienced choreographer.

Ms. Carola specializes in creative movement classes for very young children. Many of her students continue studying at the Dance Factory throughout high school, and some of these teenagers teach the younger children. The Dance Factory has a large enrollment and is now located downtown on Hamilton Street. Dianne Carola inspires her students by saying, "When dance is in you, you can't stop. If you're going to dance, you can't be a quitter."[89]

Patti Pugh Moore was a local dancer who had studied with Oleg Briansky and Phyllis Latin. After attending the North Carolina School of the Arts, she returned to Saratoga to study with Elisabeth Carroll at Skidmore College. Ms. Pugh Moore taught at Ballet Regent before opening her own studio, the

Dianne Carola teaching at her studio, the Dance Factory. *Photo by Megan Mumford.*

Children's Ballet Theatre School, in 1988. The school moved to the vacant studio space on Woodlawn Avenue when Ballet Regent moved into its own building. Patti Pugh Moore was an excellent children's teacher, and her students progressed rapidly. She soon began a small performing company, the Saratoga City Ballet, for her most advanced dancers. Patti Pugh Moore left Saratoga Springs in 2003.

The Saratoga City Ballet Company and School are under the co-direction of Julie Gedalecia and Eve Welchel. Located in the Ballet Regent Studios on Jumel Place, the school focuses on serious ballet training with additional classes in modern dance. Ms. Gedalecia has a BS in dance from Skidmore College, where she teaches as a lecturer in dance. She comments, "Teaching ballet in Saratoga is a great life. I really love it here."[90] Ms. Welchel holds a BFA from the University of Cincinnati College-Conservatory of Music and an MFA from New York University's Tisch School of the Arts. The Saratoga City Ballet School has a faculty of eight teachers who train students of all ages, and Skidmore dance faculty work with the company. Students are frequently accepted into prestigious professional ballet programs, and many are chosen to perform during the summer with the New York City Ballet. Saratoga City Ballet dancers perform an annual *Nutcracker* and spring performance at the Skidmore Dance Theater and appear at many seasonal events in Saratoga Springs.

After dancing with the New York City Ballet, Leslie Roy-Heck came to Saratoga in 1990. That same year, David Otto left the company and also moved to Saratoga. Both dancers started teaching for Ballet Regent and immediately organized a summer ballet program. The Saratoga Springs Conservatory of Dance was a five-week intensive course taught by Leslie Roy-Heck, David Otto, Michael Steele and Olga Kostritzky, with guests from the New York City Ballet. Leslie Roy-Heck soon stopped teaching ballet and chose to pursue a different path.[91]

David Otto opened the Capital Ballet Company and School in Albany. After Michael Steele's Ballet Regent closed, Otto moved his school up to Saratoga Springs and established the Saratoga Ballet Academy with his wife, Christine Otto.[92] The Ottos say, "We believe every child loves to move. Our mission is to introduce structure and technique in a caring and nurturing environment while enhancing the love of dance. We do so using the Balanchine technique which has produced some of the finest dancers in the world."[93]

Many of Otto's students attend respected professional summer programs and are chosen to appear with the New York City Ballet during their summer seasons at the Saratoga Performing Arts Center. Saratoga Ballet Academy students perform locally and at the Egg in Albany.

David Otto also teaches ballet for the Dance Department at Skidmore College. In 2011, he performed with Skidmore dancers as a guest artist in *Swan Lake, Act II,* at the Zankel Music Center.

Denise Warner Limoli joined the Skidmore dance faculty in 1992. In addition to her work at Skidmore, she immediately began teaching and staging ballets for Ballet Regent and the Saratoga City Ballet. In the community, she teaches as a private instructor and performance coach and is a member of the board of directors for the National Museum of Dance.

In 2008, the National Museum of Dance opened the School of the Arts, which offers a variety of dance styles taught by a large faculty. Although the primary focus is classical ballet, classes in modern dance, Irish step, Middle Eastern, Zumba, hip-hop and jazz are offered for students of all ages. Performances are held in the Swyer Studios and at the Spa Little Theatre.

Raul Martinez directs the school and manages the Lewis A. Swyer Studios. After graduating from the National School of Fine Arts in Mexico City, Martinez danced professionally and studied both the Vaganova and Cuban methods of ballet training. Mr. Martinez explains, "We have worked hard to establish the rigor and as high a quality as possible. It all takes time."[94]

Former principal dancer with the New York City Ballet Melinda Roy and her husband, Roberto Muñoz, are co-directors of the Saratoga Summer Dance Intensive. Originally held at the Ballet Regent studios, the program is now located in the Swyer Studios during June and July. The Saratoga program is for serious ballet students ages twelve and up, and a second program in Vail, Colorado, teaches pre-professional students starting at age fourteen. A high-caliber professional faculty teaches at both programs. Melinda Roy is the founder of the Gulfshore Ballet in Florida. She is the sister of Leslie Roy-Heck of Saratoga Springs.[95]

The most recent addition to the dance schools in Saratoga is the Myers Dance Center. Darlene Myers, who danced with the Pennsylvania Ballet Company, has been teaching ballet in Schenectady since 1985. Students of the Myers Dance Center have appeared at functions for the Saratoga Performing Arts Center, such as the Ballet Gala and the Nutcracker Tea. Select students from the Saratoga studio perform with the Northeast Ballet Company in their annual production of the *Nutcracker*.[96]

Nacre Dance Company, the resident dance company of the Universal Preservation Hall, is a professional modern dance company directed by Beth Fecteau. Nacre (French for "mother of pearl") revives and performs classic dance works by American dance pioneers, such as Doris Humphrey and Charles Weidman. The repertoire also includes original works by emerging choreographers. The dancers of Nacre offer educational programs, master classes and lecture demonstrations. Beth Fecteau states, "I resolved to create a company that would link the past with the present and carry modern dance into the future."[97]

Nacre Dance Company. *Photo by Steve J. Nealey.*

Ballroom Dance in Saratoga Springs

Ballroom dance has become very popular in Saratoga Springs. In 2005, the Arthur Murray Dance Studio moved into a customized studio in the old firehouse building on Broadway. Formerly owned and established by Leslie Ann LaGuardia, the studio offers classes in all styles of ballroom and social dance. The school's impressive roster of professional ballroom dancers and international master teachers includes Iraida Volodina of Russia, Ricardo Sopin of Haiti and the new owner and director, Safwat Gerges of Egypt.

Ms. LaGuardia won many professional ballroom competitions before leaving dance to study marketing in college. She now travels the world as public relations director, motivational speaker and coach for Arthur Murray International.

Leslie Ann LaGuardia has repeatedly won the Saratoga Springs Community Service Award for her creation of the "Pink Ball," a benefit for breast cancer research held annually at the Hall of Springs. Ms. LaGuardia and Mr. Gerges both serve on the board of directors of the National Museum of Dance. She teaches, "Instill, inspire, create. If you're born to dance, nothing gets in your way."[98]

Saratoga Savoy Center of Dance is a ballroom and social dance school directed by co-owners Keira Lemonis and David Wolf. Located on Wells Street, the school offers instruction in many styles of dance, such as swing, lindy hop, Argentine tango and hip-hop.

Dancin' Time at the Universal Preservation Hall on Washington Street also offers a variety of ballroom dance classes. This school is co-directed by Dawn and David Levesque.

Tango Fusion Dance Company and School came to Saratoga Springs in 2006 from New York City, where the company appeared at Tango Fest NYC. Co-directed by Diane Lachtrupp and Johnny Martinez, the company of ten professional dancers has performed locally at the Saratoga Performing Arts Center, Spa Little Theatre, National Museum of Dance and for the Saratoga ArtsFest. The school offers classes for adults in multiple styles of ballroom and Latin dance at its studios on Regent Street and at the Mine on Broadway. Children's classes in hip-hop, jazz, swing and salsa are held in the studio. It also directs the "Lake Ave. Swing/Salsa Kids" at the Lake Avenue Elementary School and offers a Summer Dance Camp for children at the Tango Fusion studios.[99]

OTHER ARTISTS IN THE COMMUNITY

Choreographer Debra Fernandez explains, "There is something so special about Saratoga Springs. Artists have an immediate connection here. It's so nice to be 'home.' In the 1980s, Saratoga was an eccentric, colorful town with many highly cultured people. The town was smaller than it is now, but much more sophisticated."[100] Former librarian and dance lover Rhona Koretzky-Forman declares, "This place is extraordinary."[101]

Many dance personalities and other artists in related professions have made Saratoga Springs their home. Some came to retire, but others continued their professional work. They all have made an important contribution to the rich cultural fabric of our community.

Zachary Solov (1923–2004) studied ballet with Catherine Littlefield in Philadelphia and performed with the Balanchine's Ballet Caravan, a precursor to the New York City Ballet. After serving in World War II, he returned to New York to join the American Ballet Theatre and performed on Broadway. Sir Rudolf Bing hired Solov as chief choreographer of the Metropolitan Opera, where he remained until he retired to his Victorian home in Saratoga Springs.

Solov was a gregarious person who loved to entertain with stories about his experiences in the arts. In Saratoga, he and John Martin spent time gardening and collecting antiques. Their home was filled with books and memorabilia from the ballet and the opera. The Zachary Solov Foundation preserved his collection for the New York Public Library of Performing Arts, Jerome Robbins Dance Division. After his death, a retrospective memorial to Zachary Solov was held at the Metropolitan Opera House.[102]

John Martin (1893–1985) was America's first major dance critic. He started writing with the *New York Herald Tribune* and then, in 1927, began his lengthy career with the *New York Times*. Lincoln Kirstein explained, "John Martin was practically the first, for four decades the most influential, dance critic in the United States, and historically the best informed and least self-serving."[103]

Martin was an advocate for the emerging modern dance form and championed the work of new choreographers such as Martha Graham. At the invitation of his friend Zachary Solov, John Martin moved to Saratoga Springs, where he received an honorary doctorate from Skidmore College. In 1988, he was posthumously inducted into the National Museum of Dance Hall of Fame. At a memorial for Martin, choreographer Murray Louis said, "John Martin gave the art of dance a voice at a time when it was struggling for articulation."[104]

Shaun O'Brien and Cris Alexander at Hattie's Chicken Shack in 1967. *Photo provided by Hattie's Restaurant.*

Shaun O'Brien (1925–2012) performed with the New York City Ballet for thirty-nine years and was considered one of America's great character dancers. He was best known for his portrayals of Dr. Coppélius in the ballet *Coppélia*, Herr Drosselmeyer in *Nutcracker* and the patriarch in Balanchine's *The Prodigal Son*. O'Brien came to Saratoga Springs for the New York City Ballet's first season at the Saratoga Performing Arts Center. In 1973, he and his partner, Cris Alexander, bought a house near North Broadway, where they hosted grand summer parties for dancers and fans.[105]

Cris Alexander (1920–2012) was a versatile Broadway performer who played one of the three sailors in the original Broadway cast of *On the Town*. Also a renowned photographer, Alexander was an official photographer for the New York City Ballet and worked with Andy Warhol. Alexander retired to the home he shared with Shaun O'Brien in 1993. He and O'Brien were frequently interviewed about their wonderful careers in the arts. After more than sixty years together, Shaun O'Brien and Cris Alexander died within two weeks of each other.[106]

Suzanne Ames Landry (1931–2008) was a ballerina with the Metropolitan Opera Ballet and served as vice president of EMI Music. She and her husband moved to Circular Street in Saratoga Springs after retirement.

As a volunteer for the National Museum of Dance, she gave lectures on the work of Anthony Tudor and served as a docent for many exhibits. Ms. Landry regularly attended performances and lectures and would often be seen walking downtown, which was her method of "staying young." The Suzanne Ames Landry Estate established the Performing Arts Studio at her alma mater, Our Lady of the Elms School in Akron, Ohio.[107]

Anthony Blum (1939–2000) was a principal dancer with the New York City Ballet in the 1960s and '70s who was known for a simple lyrical style. Prior to joining the company, Blum danced on Broadway and on television. When he retired from performing, Blum moved into his Saratoga cottage that he had named Dying Limbs. He worked as a designer for Lily and the Rose catering and was an avid collector of nineteenth-century bronze and pottery.[108]

Robert Maiorano was a soloist with the New York City Ballet who joined the company at the age of fifteen. He was with the company for its opening season at the Saratoga Performing Arts Center and was among the first dancers to buy a house in Saratoga Springs.

He has taught locally with Oleg Briansky, Michael Steele and Patti Pugh Moore and for the Glens Falls Dance Center, as well as with schools throughout the country. In addition to teaching ballet, Robert Maiorano pursued an eclectic career in acting, lecturing and writing. He has authored five books, including *Mozartiana: The Making of a Masterpiece* and *Worlds Apart*, an autobiography that was awarded "Best Books for Young Adults" by the American Library Association. He has also written several children's books and plays and has appeared in a variety of acting roles.

Robert Maiorano, New York City Ballet. *Photo by Michael Avedon.*

Maiorano lectures on ballet at the National Museum of Dance. He frequently hosts the Pre-Performance Talks at the Saratoga Performing Arts Center.[109]

Saratoga Dance, holiday greenery decorated with pointe shoes. *Photo provided by Leslie Roy-Heck.*

Leslie Roy-Heck was a soloist with the New York City Ballet and performed with the company for thirteen years. After her retirement from the company in 1989, Ms. Roy-Heck moved to Saratoga Springs and completed a degree from Empire State College. In 1990, she opened Saratoga Dance, a full-service professional dance supply store. Leslie and Michael Heck started their business Bunheads Dance Accessories in 1996. This enterprise soon grew to international status and has been bought by Ballet Makers, Inc./ Capezio. Ms. Roy-Heck serves on the board of directors of the National Museum of Dance.[110]

LaMar and Ruth Alsop retired to Saratoga Springs after more than forty years as musicians in the New York City Ballet Orchestra. They bought and renovated a historic property on Smith Bridge Road, where they hosted summer chamber music festivals in a custom-built concert hall on the property.

Carl Landa began as a self-taught musician and went on to earn a BA in music from Bennington College. He has played for modern dance classes at the Bates Dance Festival, at SUNY Purchase and Bennington College Dance Departments and for prominent dance companies and schools in New York City. Landa is director of music for the Skidmore College Department of

Dance, where he accompanies modern dance classes and composes for choreographers. He performs locally both as a solo jazz pianist and with his own ensemble, the Carl Landa Band. Landa explains, "Saratoga Springs became a mecca of modern dance for me and the community. I am a very lucky musician to have been exposed to and to have worked with the best, right here in Saratoga Springs."[111]

Michael Limoli is a classical clarinetist with a doctorate in music from Indiana University–Bloomington. Limoli has performed as clarinet soloist in major international venues and locally with the Saratoga Chamber Players, St. Cecilia Orchestra, Saratoga Winds and at the Music Series of both Bethesda Episcopal Church and the United Methodist Church.

Limoli is also a pianist and a former ballet dancer. In Saratoga, he has played for ballet classes at Skidmore College, New York State Summer School of the Arts School of Ballet and countless master classes and professional auditions. Michael and Denise Warner Limoli have worked together in the ballet studio as teacher and ballet pianist for over thirty years. Limoli says:

Michael and Denise Warner Limoli in the studio. *Photo provided by the Limolis.*

> *Like living in Manhattan, living in Saratoga Springs has afforded me opportunities to collaborate with many of the greatest dancers and dance teachers of our time, both as pianist and clarinetist. I am often invited to accompany master classes for visiting professional dancers and to play for major schools who make Saratoga a destination on their audition tours.*

Kim Vanyo, owner of Khymanyo Studio, is a designer of couture, bridal and dance costumes. She graduated from the Fashion Institute of Technology in New York City and moved to Saratoga Springs in 1984. Ms. Vanyo has created many costumes for the Skidmore College Dance Department, and her original designs have been featured in several collaborative performance projects at the Tang Museum and at the Zankel Music Center. Kim Vanyo declares, "Being in Saratoga Springs with its appreciation of the arts has continued to inspire new works and fields of design for me. I feel complete in that I live in beautiful Saratoga Springs, I work as a designer and continue to get interesting commissions while never ceasing to meet intriguing people."[112]

Chapter 5

The National Museum of Dance and the Mr. and Mrs. Cornelius Vanderbilt Whitney Hall of Fame

A Statement from Mrs. Marylou Whitney

Years ago during the summer, Mr. George Balanchine came to Saratoga Springs and held tryouts for aspiring ballerinas from all over New York State. He needed a place for these dancers to practice their lessons, and I believe it was originally his idea to create a dance center. One day, while sitting on my porch at Cady Hill in Saratoga Springs, Lewis Swyer and I concluded the Washington Bath House would be the perfect place for the dancers. We worked hard on the renovations in order to bring his idea to reality. In 1986, we created the National Museum of Dance, a place that had wonderful exhibits of old dance costumes, pictures and memorabilia. It was also a place where aspiring dancers could practice in the studios and attend lessons with renowned dancers from the New York City Ballet.

I was president of the board of directors for a while, but as time went on, I turned the position over to many other people who were interested in dance; however, it always seemed to be running in the red. When I first met Michele Riggi, she told me she was a dancer and loved the museum. Michele wanted to be involved, so she took over as president of the board of directors and has made more progress than all of us combined. Michele brought the museum to life. She has successfully accomplished what Lewis Swyer and I aspired to do years ago. As long as Michele Riggi is at the museum, it will thrive. It makes me so happy to see what the National Museum of Dance is today because of all her great work and efforts.[113]

THE VISION AND THE RENOVATION

Visionary: a person of strong and creative imaginative power and, often, the ability to inspire others.[114]

The concept of a museum for dance and the ultimate realization of the National Museum of Dance and Hall of Fame were due to the passionate dedication and perseverance of the late Lewis A. Swyer and Mrs. Marylou Whitney. Both were visionaries with a genuine love of dance.

The historic Washington Bath House in Saratoga Spa Park had fallen into serious disrepair. Saratoga community leaders agreed that something needed to be done to save such an important building. Two gentlemen from the Saratoga Performing Arts Center—Lewis Swyer, the chairman of the board, and executive director Herb Chesbrough—approached Marylou and Cornelius Vanderbilt Whitney with an idea. They proposed to turn the building into a dance museum. This museum would enhance the presence

Mr. and Mrs. Cornelius Vanderbilt Whitney and Lewis A. Swyer with the model of the National Museum of Dance. *Photo courtesy of the National Museum of Dance.*

of the New York City Ballet at the Saratoga Performing Arts Center while furthering the reputation of Saratoga Springs as a destination for world-class dance. The Whitneys approved of the idea.

The story is reminiscent of the founding of the Saratoga Performing Arts Center itself. Lewis A. Swyer Co., Inc., had built the amphitheater. Swyer's construction expertise enabled him to guide every detail of the demolition and renovation of the Washington Bath House. Lewis Swyer envisioned three phases of development: first, the exhibit spaces; second, a lecture hall and a resource library; and third, a studio building for the New York State Summer School of the Arts Schools of Ballet and Dance, where the public could observe dancers practicing their art. The Whitneys provided much of the project's initial funding. Mrs. Whitney oversaw many details with great interest, particularly the restoration of the foyer, and she frequently brought her guests to observe the progress. She wanted to make sure that everyone knew that Saratoga Springs was the home of the only museum dedicated to performance dance in the country.[115]

After the initial construction began, an article describing the project was printed in the *New York Times*, and a sign appeared on the lawn: "National Museum of Dance coming soon." Alison Moore, a Skidmore alumna working for the director of arts for the State University of New York, read that article and was intrigued by the concept. She submitted a five-year plan to Chesbrough and Swyer, and in January 1986, Alison Moore was hired as the museum's first director.[116]

The word was out, and excited dance lovers from around the area began volunteering in any way they could. Sharon Walsh, a local arts administrator, volunteered to work for the new museum:

> *Alison Moore and I struck an immediate simpatico, and we began to visualize the potential exhibit spaces. We made an incredibly long list of what had to happen for the museum; we divided and conquered, and we made it all happen. The volunteers were probably the most interesting group of people that ever came together to do anything. Everyone wanted this to happen, so they were willing to do anything, from drawing posters to hammering nails. Everyone worked 24/7, and no one said no to any request; we simply got it done.*[117]

It took many hands to realize this dream. The list of volunteers included dozens of dedicated dance fans, too numerous to mention. The leaders of the local dance community—Pat Peterson, founder of the Dance Alliance, and Mary DiSanto-Rose and Isabel Brown of Skidmore College—lent valuable expertise.

While the interior construction work was underway, Alison Moore and Sharon Walsh worked off-site at the administrative offices of the Saratoga Performing Arts Center. As the interior gallery spaces began to take shape, they worked together to articulate the museum's artistic mission. The museum would focus on educating the public about the rich history of performance dance in America, not just ballet and modern dance but tap, jazz and ethnic forms as well. The aim was to create more appreciative audiences, more dancers and more creative opportunities for choreographers.[118]

Alison Moore said, "We insisted on nothing but the best. I knew a lot of people, so I called on the experts. We had to be endlessly creative, with a shoestring budget, but we were determined to create a place of excellence."[119] Ms. Moore sought out advice and participation from such colleagues as arts writer Mindy Aloff, Genevieve Oswald of the New York Public Library for the Performing Arts Dance Collection, Marty Bronson of the Fashion Institute of Technology and the historian and archivist of Jacob's Pillow Dance Festival, Norton Owen.

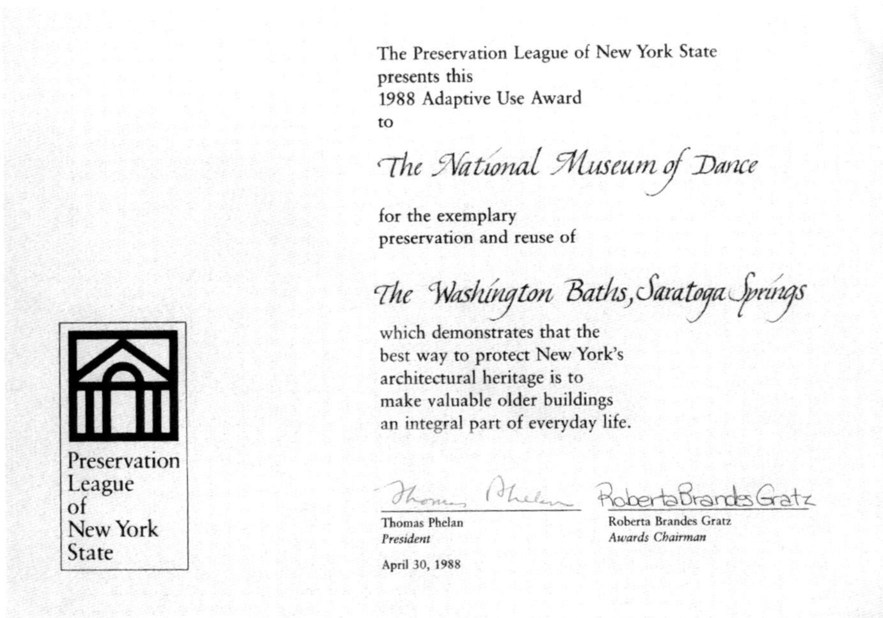
The Preservation League of New York State
presents this
1988 Adaptive Use Award
to

The National Museum of Dance

for the exemplary
preservation and reuse of

The Washington Baths, Saratoga Springs

which demonstrates that the
best way to protect New York's
architectural heritage is to
make valuable older buildings
an integral part of everyday life.

Preservation League of New York State

Thomas Phelan
President

Roberta Brandes Gratz
Awards Chairman

April 30, 1988

Award for renovation of the Washington Bath House. *Courtesy of the National Museum of Dance.*

In 1988, the Preservation League of New York State presented the Adaptive Use Award to the museum for the "exemplary preservation and reuse of the Washington Baths, Saratoga Springs."[120]

THE NATIONAL MUSEUM OF DANCE OPENS ITS DOORS

The National Museum of Dance opened with a preview season in July 1986. Initial exhibits included "Dressing the Ballet," a large collection of costumes from the signature repertoire of major ballet companies, and William Ewing's "Dance and Photography," a collection of the work of great twentieth-century dance photographers.

Sharon Walsh remembers, "The numbers in the summer months were staggering. We couldn't believe it! The people of Saratoga Springs, dance lovers and those who were simply curious poured into the museum. Busloads of tourists en route to Saratoga Performing Arts Center stopped at the museum."[121] To accommodate visitors, a volunteer docent program was quickly established to guide people through the exhibits. At the Saratoga Performing Arts Center, the museum docents gave lectures, held conversations with New York City Ballet dancers and conducted tours of the back stage area of the amphitheater.

By 1990, the National Museum of Dance had completed the gallery spaces, and several important new exhibits were opened. "The Fugitive Gesture" was a collection of images by major twentieth-century dance photographers. "Les Ballets 1933" was an exhibit on George Balanchine's first company in the West, obtained from London and curated by Jane Pritchard; "100 Years of Russian Ballet" was a touring exhibit from Leningrad and obtained through Washington, D.C. Alison Moore and her staff, the board of directors and dedicated volunteers had all made a huge statement: "The National Museum of Dance represents the highest level of professional dance in America, and we are here to stay."[122]

In the early 1990s, Alison Moore left to pursue other artistic challenges. She was succeeded by a series of directors, each of whom worked to ensure that quality exhibits and Hall of Fame inductions continued. The exhibits "Ted Shawn, the Father of American Dance"; "Bronislava Nijinska: Classic on the Edge"; and "Classic Black: African American Dancers in Classical Ballet" were among the highlights of the 1990s. Featured during the 2000s were "An

From the exhibit "Classic Black," Ms. Doris Jones of the Jones-Hayward School and students. *Photo courtesy of the National Museum of Dance.*

American Mosaic: Dance Photos by Steven Caras"; "The Enduring Legacy of George Balanchine: Balanchine in Saratoga"; and "On Broadway!"

The Modern Dance Festivals at the Spa Little Theatre were bringing important modern dance companies to Saratoga Springs. The companies enhanced the museum's exhibits by offering lecture-demonstrations of works choreographed by many Hall of Fame honorees.

President Michele Riggi, Director Donna Skiff and Assistant Director Sarah Hall-Weaver. *Photo by Tammy Loya.*

After years of experience in other capacities at the museum, Donna Skiff became the director in 2008. Ms. Skiff declares, "The National Museum of Dance is always going to be a small museum, but that doesn't mean it can't be a great museum."[123] Along with Ms. Skiff came a young staff that has matured into capable professionals. Michele Riggi began as president of the board of directors and reorganized the board to include former professional dancers among its ranks. A dynamic new dance museum team was formed.

Recent major exhibits include "100 Years of the Ballets Russes"; "Eleo Pomare: The Man, the Artist, the Maker of Artists"; and "American Ballet Theatre: Then and Now." A complete renovation of the Hall of Fame is underway, and there are plans for the building of a theater for films and lectures.

Most nonprofit arts organizations have relied on volunteers. Countless local dance lovers have offered their time and talents to the National Museum of Dance, some working in the lobby gift shop and others helping with preparations for special programs. Heather Mabee, a past president of

"American Ballet Theatre: Then and Now," exhibit curated by Denise Warner Limoli. *Photo by Francesca Limoli.*

the board, said, "The very core of the museum during those unstable years was the dedication of the docents and volunteers who kept the museum alive and open."[124]

Two local women stand out for their dedication to the museum: Mary Ann Fantauzzi and Susan Edwards. Both have been at the museum since the beginning, working beside Sharon Walsh and Alison Moore. Ms. Fantauzzi volunteers as a docent and writes the docent educational guides for the exhibits. Susan Edwards is now the program director and works in the Resource Room. She explains, "I have stayed because I cannot give up being a part of what we started. It's sort of a guardianship if situations are detrimental, or a sharing in all of the amazing growth and importance we have achieved."[125]

EDUCATION AND OUTREACH PROGRAMS

The Resource Room at the National Museum of Dance houses a substantial digitalized collection of dance books, periodicals, performance programs and posters. This collection is available for public browsing and for academic research.

A recent designated gift has allowed the museum to begin work on an Archive Room with proper light, temperature and humidity controls. The museum's bequest collections, videos, costumes, photos and other memorabilia will be safely stored and catalogued in this new facility.

A children's wing opened in 2007, complete with costumes, barres and mirrors and a small stage for budding performers. This important educational facility was renovated and reopened in 2011. Thanks to a generous grant, the Alfred Z. Solomon Children's Wing enabled greatly expanded programming that included vacation dance camps, children's art exhibits and special workshops for local students.

The excellent programing at the National Museum of Dance helps to demonstrate that this is a museum for all types of people to enjoy learning about all styles of dance. Film showings, book signings, lectures, dance parties, and performances in the Swyer Studios are only some of the successful events that help increase public awareness, visibility and participation.

To highlight a unique exhibit of international dance, "Postage Paid," the museum hosted several cultural festivals. India Day, Greek Day, Hispanic Day, Italy Day and others were public events that celebrated the cultures through their dance, music, art and food. The annual celebration of National Dance Day has attracted large numbers to the museum for the fun of moving and dancing together. Well over two hundred people came for the Black History Month Celebration. Dancers' Health Day brought together several top professionals in the health, nutrition and fitness fields to speak about the specific needs of dancers' bodies. For the exhibit "En Pointe," a pointe shoe–decorating contest inspired young and old alike to submit dozens of elaborately embellished shoes.[126]

The National Museum of Dance celebrated its twenty-fifth anniversary in 2011. Many people returned to the museum for the event, including Alison Moore and other former directors. Ms. Moore exclaimed, "I am so thrilled the National Museum of Dance still exists and happy that people are working so hard to keep it going."[127] Everyone present was gratified to

India Day dancers Francesca Limoli and Rosalind Elliot and musicians Veena Chandra, Devesh Chandra and Jessica Taffet. *Photo by Ruby Whitney.*

see that the National Museum of Dance is thriving and well on the way to becoming a preeminent source for educating the public and showcasing all styles of dance.

THE BOARD OF DIRECTORS

The members of the board of directors of the National Museum of Dance have been prominent dance enthusiasts who have come together to support this unique museum. Mrs. Marylou Whitney and Lewis Swyer both served for many years, and second-generation Whitneys and Swyers have followed in their parents' footsteps. Mrs. Heather (Whitney) Mabee was president of the board for six years. She commented, "My parents had a tremendous love of dance. I felt I had to continue their legacy."[128]

There has always been a member of the Swyer family on the board of directors. Museum founder Lewis Swyer served until his death in

1988 and was followed by his son Edward Swyer, who served from 1988 to 2002. Carol Swyer replaced her brother and is still an active board member. Both have worked to honor their father's vision and dedication to dance. Carol Swyer explains:

> *My father, Lewis A. Swyer, was a force! He was passionate about the arts, especially dance. He knew how to get things done, and I grew up watching him make things happen. When my father walked me through this abandoned, deteriorating bath house, I saw that sparkle in his eyes as he envisioned his dream of a museum devoted solely to dance, and I had no doubt that it would become a reality. He passed his passion—the love of dance—on to me. It is a privilege to continue the Swyer family's support of the National Museum of Dance.*[129]

The current president of the board of directors is Michele Riggi, a former dancer, performer and dance teacher. Ms. Riggi has worked tirelessly to increase the museum's membership and visibility. As president, Ms. Riggi formed an excellent working board of professionals with diverse specialties. Under her leadership, the annual galas have brought exciting dance personalities to our community. These summer events have become the primary source of funding for the museum.

In 2011, Michele Riggi and the National Museum of Dance were honored for "Contributions to the World of Dance" at the Career Transitions for Dancers annual benefit in New York City.[130]

> *I have a real passion for dance. The National Museum of Dance now has a dynamic Board of Directors and a wonderful staff. We all share the same passion, the same dream, the same vision. We must continue this model because it makes the National Museum of Dance strong. We are moving forward! There were important women from the past I never got to know—Pat Peterson, Mae Banner, Alison Moore—who had a profound effect on the museum, and I wish they could have mentored me. I am so fortunate to have my dear friend Mrs. Mary Lou Whitney as my mentor and inspiration. I am proud to continue her vision and dream, and I work for the National Museum of Dance in her honor.*[131]

THE MR. AND MRS. CORNELIUS VANDERBILT WHITNEY HALL OF FAME

The Hall of Fame at the National Museum of Dance was named to honor the philanthropists who believed so strongly in the value of the museum. The Mr. and Mrs. Cornelius Vanderbilt Whitney Hall of Fame opened in the summer of 1987. The first group of honorees was inducted at a ceremony attended by those whose hard work made the dream a reality. The original honoree exhibit in the area adjoining the Hall of Fame was titled, "Shaping the American Dance Dream."

A number of Hall of Fame honorees, such as Merce Cunningham, Paul Taylor and Trisha Brown, were inducted while their modern dance companies were performing in Saratoga Springs.

Candidates for the Mr. and Mrs. Cornelius Vanderbilt Whitney Hall of Fame are nominated by a national committee. The nominating committee includes all living honorees, professional dance directors, historians, dance writers and professors. An effort is made to balance the variety of disciplines represented, and both posthumous and living candidates are considered. Honorees represent a variety of professionals who have made a major impact on dance in America. The chosen nominee is ultimately confirmed by the entire board of directors.

NATIONAL MUSEUM OF DANCE

Honorees of the Cornelius Vanderbilt Whitney Hall of Fame

<u>1987</u>
Fred Astaire (1899–1987)
George Balanchine (1904–1983)
Agnes DeMille (1905–1993)
Isadora Duncan (1877–1927)
Katherine Dunham (1909–2006)
Martha Graham (1894–1991)
Doris Humphrey (1895–1958)
Lincoln Kirstein (1907–1996)
Catherine Littlefield (1905–1951)
Bill "Bojangles" Robinson (1878–1949)
Ted Shawn (1891–1972)

The Leland Opera House. *Saratoga Room Collection, Saratoga Springs Public Library.*

Souvenir program of the first Floral Fête, 1894. *Saratoga Room Collection, Saratoga Springs Public Library.*

Souvenir program of the third Floral Fête, 1896. *Saratoga Room Collection, Saratoga Springs Public Library.*

Missa Brevis choreography by José Limón, performed by the José Limón Dance Company with Skidmore dancers outside in the Surrey Gardens. *Photo by Steve J. Nealey.*

Bharatanatyam dancer, Francesca Limoli (2012). *Photo by Sam Brook.*

Finding Balance choreography by Mary Harney. *Photo by Gosh Gerritson.*

Tempus Fugit choreography by Denise Warner Limoli. *Photo by Steve J. Nealey.*

Balls choreography by Debra J. Fernandez. *Photo by Steve J. Nealey.*

Keeping Company with Cage choreography by Debra J. Fernandez. *Photo by Sam Brook.*

Swan Lake, Act II staged by Denise Warner Limoli. *Photo by Steve J. Nealey.*

Complete This Work Which We Began choreography and film by Rubén Graciani. *Photo by Erin Kobor.*

"Steps in the Street" from *Chronicle* choreography by Martha Graham. *Photo by Joe Ritter.*

Mary Collins of Schenectady poses backstage with Edward Villella before *Harlequinade,* choreography by George Balanchine. ©The George Balanchine Trust. *Photo provided by Mary (Collins) Harney.*

Skidmore dancers prepare for a performance at Kaatsbaan International Dance Center. *Photo by Mary DiSanto-Rose.*

At night on the lawn of the Saratoga Performing Arts Center. *Photo provided by the Saratoga Performing Arts Center.*

Students of the Saratoga City Ballet School. *Photo provided by Julie Gedalecia.*

Above: Students from the Saratoga Ballet Academy. *Victorian Sketches* by director David Otto. *Photo by Teresa Zielinsky.*

Right: Denise Warner Limoli, American Ballet Theatre. *Photo by J. Heffernan.*

Left: Iraida Volodina and Ricardo Sopin of Arthur Murray Dance Studio. *Photo provided by Leslie Anne LaGuardia.*

Below: Kim Vanyo of Khymanyo Studio designing the tutu for *Firebird*. *Photo by Raul Martinez.*

The National Museum of Dance. The sculpture on the front lawn was given to the National Museum of Dance by Mrs. Ann Swyer in 1989. Sculpture *Athena* by Judith Brown. *Photo by Ruby Whitney.*

National Museum of Dance foyer and Hall of Fame. *Photo by Ruby Whitney.*

Rehearsal of *Apollo* for Saratoga Dances II. *Photo by Anthony Tassarotti. Apollo* choreography by George Balanchine. ©*The George Balanchine Trust.*

New York City Ballet dancers relax onstage at Zankel Music Center during rehearsal for Saratoga Dances II. *Photo by Anthony Tassarotti.*

Nacre Dance Company. *Photo by Steve J. Nealey.*

Swan Song choreography by Debra J. Fernandez, Saratoga ArtsFest. *Photo by Steve J. Nealey.*

Da Pacem by Denise Warner Limoli. *Photo by Steve J. Nealy.*

Michele and Ronald Riggi. *Photo by Imagine! Photography.*

By Ruben Graciani. *Photo by Steve J. Nealy.*

Saratoga City Ballet in *The Nutcracker. Photo by John Sullivan.*

New York City Ballet ballerina Violette Verdy poses at the construction site of the Saratoga Performing Arts Center. *Photo by Martha Swope.*

Ruth St. Denis (1879–1968)
Charles Weidman (1901–1975)

<u>1988</u>
Busby Berkeley (1895–1976)
Lucia Chase (1897–1986)
Hanya Holm (1893–1992)
John Martin (1893–1985)
Anthony Tudor (1908–1987)

<u>1989</u>
Jerome Robbins (1918–1998)

<u>1992</u>
Alvin Ailey (1931–1989)

<u>1993</u>
Merce Cunningham (1919–2009)

<u>1994</u>
Bronislava Nijinska (1891–1972)

<u>1995</u>
Paul Taylor (1930–)

<u>1997</u>
José Limón (1908–1972)

<u>1998</u>
Anna Sokolow (1910–2000)

<u>1999</u>
Barbara Karinska (1886–1983)
Arthur Mitchell (1934–)

<u>2000</u>
Trisha Brown (1936–)
Robert Joffrey (1930–1988)
Alwin Nikolais (1910–1993)

2001
Fayard Nicholas (1914–2006)
Harold Nicholas (1921–2000)

2002
Edwin Denby (1903–1983)
Leonide Massine (1896–1979)

2004
Igor Stravinsky (1882–1971)

2006
Arthur and Kathryn Murray
The New Dance Group (1932)

2007
Bob Fosse (1927–1987)
Bill T. Jones (1952–)

2008
Peter Martins (1946–)

2009
Marge Champion (1919–)
Suzanne Farrell (1945–)
Frankie Manning (1914–2009)
Tommy Tune (1939–)
Edward Villella (1936–)

2010
Michael Jackson (1958–2009)

2011
Frederic Franklin (1914–)
Oliver Smith (1918–1994)

2012
Ben Vereen (1946–)

2013
Judith Jamison (1943–)
Anna Pavlova (1881–1931)

THE LEWIS A. SWYER SCHOOL FOR THE PERFORMING ARTS

Edward Swyer said of his father, "He felt that dance was the most creative, the most noble of the performing arts. If you couldn't dance, you could do the next best thing; that is, appreciate and support it."[132]

Lewis Swyer's vision was that of a living dance museum, not just a static collection of exhibits and galleries. He imagined a location where the public could observe dance in progress—the training, the rehearsals and the creative process. His dream was realized one year after his death, when the L.A. Swyer Company began construction of the Lewis A. Swyer Dance Studios, located directly behind the museum. To complement the beautiful museum building, the studios were also designed and built in the Craftsman style.[133] This $1 million structure housed three state-of-the-art studios with flexible walls, marley-covered sprung floors, sound systems and observation windows for the public. Ample dressing rooms and a central lounge area for dancers and visitors completed the facility.

Lewis A. Swyer (1918–1988). *Courtesy of the Swyer family.*

The Lewis A. Swyer School for the Performing Arts opened in 1992. The facility became the home of the New York State Summer School of the Arts Schools of Ballet and Modern Dance. Auditions, master classes, lectures and demonstrations by visiting companies were also held there.

The School of the Arts, a program of the National Museum of Dance, opened in the Swyer Studios in 2008. Headed by Raul Martinez, a large faculty teaches classical ballet and a unique variety of styles of dance to appeal to dancers of all ages and experience levels. The vitality of the School of the Arts ensures that the National Museum of Dance is a living museum where hundreds of students are dancing.

One of the most influential business leaders in the region, Lewis A. Swyer was a passionate advocate for the arts, especially dance. His construction company built the Saratoga Performing Arts Center. Swyer joined the board of directors in 1968 and served as chairman and president of the Saratoga Performing Arts Center from 1974 until 1988. He also envisioned and co-founded the National Museum of Dance, where the Lewis A. Swyer School for the Performing Arts was built and named in his honor. In 2012, Lewis Swyer's legacy was celebrated with an engraved star on the Saratoga Performing Arts Center Walk of Fame.

Chapter 6

The Office of Special Programs, Skidmore College

On the old campus, Skidmore College had few programs that regularly utilized the facilities during the summer. Oleg Briansky's summer ballet school was among the first in the 1960s. After the North Broadway campus opened, Skidmore organized the Office of Special Programs to identify and solicit a variety of quality programs. Originally, this office was to administer all programs and residencies on campus during the summer, but its responsibilities quickly expanded to year-round activities.

Modern Dance Summer Residencies

In 1984, Beverly D'Anne of the New York State Council on the Arts met with Professor Mary DiSanto-Rose, Pat Peterson and Donald McCormack. They discussed the possibility of establishing a new residency program on campus that would enable New York modern dance companies to reach upstate communities. The Office of Special Programs chose the José Limón Dance Company for its first six-week summer dance residency. In addition to helping the company create the curriculum, Summer Programs managed all student registration, housing, meals and transportation. The success of this initial program led to an annual summer modern dance residency program at Skidmore College.

Mark Morris with Skidmore dance major Cristina Arés (1996). *Photo by Emma Dodge Hanson.*

For three weeks in June, visiting modern dance companies create new works and teach technique classes, repertory and choreography. In many cases, college students who participate in the program have the option to receive academic credit. Students are permitted to observe the professional dancers in rehearsals, and they attend the company's lecture demonstrations and performances. At the end of the session, students present a public showing of the repertoire they have learned and a sampling of their own choreography.

Skidmore College has gained considerable prestige due to the relationship it has developed with many of the modern dance choreographers and dance companies of the twentieth and early twenty-first centuries. The list of these resident companies includes virtually all the major names and creative pioneers of modern dance. Some of these companies have returned to campus for several summers, and many participated in the Department of Dance's January program.[134]

Skidmore Special Programs has brought together artists from different disciplines and has encouraged collaboration among them while they are on campus. For example, Garth Fagan's full-length work *Griot* was created with trumpeter Winton Marsalis. Ronald K. Brown dancers performed with jazz singer Nnenna Freelon. In 2012, Bill T. Jones dancers and Anne

Bill T. Jones with summer modern dance program scholarship students. *Photo by Maria McColl.*

Bogart's SITI Company actors presented *Rite of Spring*, a work in progress to commemorate the 100th anniversary of the ballet.

Three of the resident choreographers used their time on campus to develop major dance works for Broadway. Bill T. Jones worked on his award winning show, *Fela!*, Garth Fagan choreographed sections of *The Lion King* and Lar Lubovich created much of *The Red Shoes* while their companies were at Skidmore.

In the early 2000s, the McCormack Visiting Artist-Scholar in Residence was established. During the fall and spring semesters, artists have interacted directly with students and faculty by giving lectures, readings, showings and performances. Thus far, two dancers have been engaged for this prestigious residency. Dancer and choreographer Trisha Brown presented "Dance and Art," a collaborative project at the Tang Museum. Skidmore's curriculum program for all freshmen, First Year Experience, incorporated the dance and writings of choreographer Bill T. Jones. At the time, he was preparing *Fondly Do We Hope...Fervently Do We Pray*, a major dance-theater piece inspired by Abraham Lincoln. All freshmen students shared readings, viewings and a lecture presentation with Jones.[135]

The Office of Special Programs administers all conferences and a multitude of other activities throughout the year. In the summer of 2008, the Society of Dance History Scholars Thirty-first Annual Conference was co-hosted by the Dance Department and Special Programs. Dance faculty and several dance alumni presented a panel on the evolution of dance at Skidmore College and the impact dance at Skidmore has had on their lives.

A CREATIVE STAFF

Site-specific dance at the Tang Museum during the residency of the Martha Graham Dance Company. *Photo provided by the Office of Special Programs.*

The two primary visionaries of the nationally recognized Office of Special Programs at Skidmore College are Sharon Arpey and Donald McCormack. Sharon Arpey is a forty-year veteran of Special Programs and is currently the program director. Ms. Arpey is responsible for conference operations, institutes and programs and the management of the summer campus, including the modern dance residencies. Maria McColl is the Assistant Director of Institutes and Programs and facilitates the dance residencies. Antoinette Smith consults with the visiting dance companies to create the course curriculum for all credit-bearing residencies.

Donald McCormack started working for Special Programs in 1972. He became dean in 1986 and steered the program until his retirement almost twenty years later. He worked as a tireless advocate for the arts and education, and he was dedicated to bringing the best to Skidmore and introducing them to the surrounding community. His vast contacts ranged from choreographers to musicians, from writers to stage directors and everything in between.

Since Donald McCormack's retirement, there have been several deans, including Paula Newberg (2005–6), Jeffrey Segrave (2006–11) and interim dean Paul Calhoun who began in 2011.[136]

Skidmore's Office of Special Programs has been greatly responsible for exposing upstate New York to modern dance and has had an important impact on cultural life in Saratoga Springs. Partly as a result of this exposure, other venues in the area established modern dance series, such as the Egg in Albany and the Spa Little Theatre. Some modern dance companies have been presented on the Saratoga Performing Arts Center main stage. The Dance Alliance, the National Museum of Dance and the Saratoga ArtsFest have all collaborated with and benefitted from the dance residencies sponsored by the Office of Special Programs at Skidmore College.

Chapter 7

Modern Dance in Saratoga Springs

Festivals at the Spa Little Theatre

Under the auspices of the Saratoga Performing Arts Center, the Spa Little Theatre has long been one of the primary presenters of modern dance in Saratoga Springs. Its smaller stage and more manageable seating capacity have made the Little Theatre a better-suited venue for modern dance than the large amphitheater. Small-scale ballet performances were also held there.

In the summer of 1969, dancer and choreographer Paul Sanasardo began the Theatre of Modern Dance, a festival of modern dance performances and a school for dance students. Sanasardo and many of the performing artists were part of a teaching faculty that included Dance Alliance founder Patricia Peterson, Skidmore's Isabel Brown and Mary DiSanto-Rose. This festival was held in August, from 1969 to 1972, and featured a selection of the prominent modern dance companies of the time. Many of these dance companies were also performing nearby at Jacob's Pillow Dance Festival in Becket, Massachusetts.[137]

For a few years, the Acting Company and Film Festival dominated the Spa Little Theatre. Dance returned briefly in 1975 with performances by the Murray Lewis Dance Company, and from 1979 to 1983, modern dance programing was reinstated.

The 1980s were an important decade for modern dance in Saratoga Springs. In 1984, Skidmore College Special Programs started the modern

The Spa Little Theatre. *Photo provided by the Saratoga Performing Arts Center.*

dance residencies on campus, the National Museum of Dance opened in 1987 and the New York State Summer School of the Arts School of Dance began its program in 1988. The Little Theatre Modern Dance Festivals resumed in the late 1980s with the return of many favorites, the introduction of several new companies and a variety of other dance styles.

The New York City Ballet's Little Theatre Choreography Project, directed by Sean Lavery, debuted in the Little Theatre during the 1987 and 1988 seasons. Young dancers from the School of American Ballet performed in informal lecture demonstrations that introduced several young choreographers to a new audience. Also during the 1989 season, the Copasetics, a classic jazz tap group from Harlem, and Flamenco dancer Pilar Rioja performed.

The extensive 1988 and 1989 modern dance seasons included performances of well-known works and Saratoga premiers. Many of the companies participated in lecture/demonstrations and master classes at the National Museum of Dance, and several of these great choreographers were inducted into the Hall of Fame while their companies were performing in Saratoga Springs.[138]

"Dance Views" was a 1991 series of "informances." Companies showed their work in an informal setting and discussed the creative process with audiences. Participants included Lar Lubovich Dance Company, Garth Fagan Dance and the Denishawn Repertory Dancers.[139]

As a result of the modern dance festivals in the Spa Little Theatre, the preeminent modern dance companies of the country developed strong ties to Saratoga Springs. Together, the Saratoga Performing Arts Center and Skidmore College were striving to establish a modern dance season to complement that of the New York City Ballet. Saratoga Springs was indeed becoming a destination for world-class dance.

SARATOGA PERFORMING ARTS CENTER

By the late 1990s, select modern dance companies were moving onto the main stage of the amphitheater. Garth Fagan Dance Company performed *Griot*, a work created with musician Wynton Marsalis and a varied repertory program. Writer Mae Banner, an avid modern dance fan, wrote:

Bill T. Jones/Arnie Zane Dance Company. *Fondly Do We Hope…Fervently Do We Pray* choreography by Bill T. Jones. *Photo by Lawrence White courtesy of Saratoga Performing Arts Center.*

> *"Translation" was smooth, never frantic, loose but controlled, with the beat deep down in it. It finished with an easy strut that crowded the stage with leg-thrusting, shoulder-swiveling groups, so joyous that the crowd clapped the beat while the dancers did it all over again for a rousing curtain call.*[140]

More recently, Bill T. Jones/Arnie Zane Dance Company performed Jones's dance-theater work *Fondly Do We Hope…Fervently Do We Pray* and a repertory program featuring one of his signature pieces, *Dead Man in the Water*. Other major modern dance companies—Martha Graham Dance Company, Trisha Brown Dance Company, Mark Morris Dance Group, Paul Taylor Dance Company and José Limón Dance Company—have all performed on the main stage. Mae Banner again commented:

> *When the Limón Company dances, the center holds. This is so, whether it's a solo or an ensemble dance. Even when the ensemble angles off into couples or quartets, the invisible center draws them like a magnet, grounding their most far-flung forays.*[141]

Ellen Sinopoli Dance Company. *Rising Low* choreography by Ellen Sinopoli. *Photo by Gary Gold.*

There are currently two modern dance companies in the area. Nacre is the company in residence at the Universal Preservation Hall in Saratoga Springs. Directed by Beth Fecteau, Nacre presents classic modern works and showcases new choreographers from the area. The Ellen Sinopoli Dance Company is the resident company at the Egg in Albany and frequently performs in Saratoga Springs.

The Saratoga Performing Arts Center and Skidmore College have led the way by promoting modern dance in Saratoga Springs. Joined by the National Museum of Dance, New York State Summer School of the Arts and the efforts of the Dance Alliance and Saratoga ArtsFest, there is a substantial interrelated modern dance presence in the capital district. Regional presenters, such as the Egg, Jacob's Pillow Dance Festival and Kaatsbaan International Dance Center enable the companies to reach a wider audience in the Capital District.

Spa Little Theatre

1969–1972

Alvin Ailey Dance Company
Dance Theatre of Harlem
Lucas Hoving Dance Company
Murray Lewis Dance Company
Paul Sanasardo Dance Company
Paul Taylor Dance Company
Philobulus
Repertory Dance Theatre of Utah

1979–1983

Alvin Aliley American Dance Company
5 by 2 Plus Dance Company
José Limón Dance Company
Lar Lubovich Dance Company
Mummenschanz
Nikolais Dance Theatre
Twyla Tharp Dance Foundation

1986–1990

Hubbard Street Dance Company
Laura Dean Dancers and Musicians
Lewitzky Dance Company
Liz Lerman Dance Exchange
Mark Morris Dance Group
Merce Cunningham Dance Company
Murray Lewis Dance Company
Nicholas Rodriguez and DanceCompass
Nikolais Dance Theatre
Paul Taylor Dance Company
Susan Marshall and Company
Trisha Brown Company

Twyla Tharp Dance
Urban Bush Women

Saratoga Performing Arts Center

1990s–2012

Bill T. Jones/Arnie Zane Dance Company
Garth Fagan Dance
José Limón Dance Company
Mark Morris Dance Group
Martha Graham Dance Company
Paul Taylor Dance Company
Trisha Brown Dance Company

Chapter 8

Dance Organizations in Saratoga Springs

The Dance Alliance

Pat Peterson was considered to be the guiding spirit and matriarch of the capital district dance community. She started and developed the dance department at the Emma Willard School in Troy. After her retirement from the school, the Pat Peterson Dance Scholarship was established to recognize an outstanding Emma Willard dance student. Pat then devoted all her time to developing dance audiences, volunteering at the National Museum of Dance and directing the Dance Alliance.[142]

Patricia Peterson (1925–2011). *Photo provided by Mary Disanto-Rose.*

Under the leadership of Pat Peterson, a community of dance professionals, dance enthusiasts and arts administrators came together in 1978 to form the Dance Alliance. This membership organization was created to facilitate the sharing of information about dance activities in the area. They produced a monthly newsletter that listed all dance opportunities from local performances and master classes to calls for choreographers and trips to Jacob's Pillow Dance Festival. The Dance Alliance has subsequently become a primary resource for information and support of the myriad dance-related events in Saratoga Springs.[143]

EDUCATIONAL PROGRAMS

The Dance Alliance sponsors educational programs that utilize the multiple dance resources in Saratoga Springs. Begun in 1990 by former Skidmore dance pianist Judith Fitzner-Atchinson, the annual Dance+ Festival is a weekend of diverse dance classes for students of all abilities and all ages. Local and invited guest teachers give classes in ballet, tap, classical Indian dance, modern dance and other styles. After being hosted by the Skidmore Dance Department for twenty years, Dance+ is now a one-day event held in the Swyer Studios at the National Museum of Dance.

Andrew Scordato teaching for Saratoga Community Day. *Photo by Anthony Tassarotti.*

Dancing Through Time is a dance sampler series for senior citizens, also held in the Swyer Studios. Dance professionals offer a lecture presentation on a specific style or choreographer followed by a movement class based on that type of dance. Topics include the legacy of Anthony Tudor, works of Agnes DeMille, the design art of the Ballets Russes and many others.

The Saratoga Community Day has introduced dancers in the community to a variety of dance professionals who teach master classes and discuss their careers. The most recent guest was Andrew Scordato from the New York City Ballet.[144]

Dance Alliance has organized trips to dance performances at Jacob's Pillow Dance Festival in Massachusetts, The Egg in Albany, Proctor's Theatre in Schenectady, EMPAC in Troy and to theaters in New York City. It co-sponsors dance events with the National Museum of Dance, the Emma Willard School and area colleges. This sharing of resources enables visiting artists to "tour" throughout the region.

The Pat and Sven Peterson Scholarship is awarded to a young dance student for intensive summer study. The applicants are screened by members of a selection committee, and the student must be a member of the Dance Alliance.[145]

The late Pat Peterson's vision galvanized a dynamic group of dance enthusiasts. They have since been led by former president Mary DiSanto-Rose and current president Mary Ann Fantauzzi. The Dance Alliance members endeavor to fulfill the organization's original mission:

> *To create an atmosphere in which dance will flourish by networking and sharing resources among its members; by supporting a critical process for choreographers, performers, and audience, by sponsoring alone or in collaboration with other institutions, dance education programs and concerts for its membership and the public at large.*[146]

SARATOGA DANCES I AND II

In keeping with the mission for Dance Alliance to support emerging choreographers, a major new initiative, Saratoga Dances, is underway. Saratoga Dances celebrates the continuing relationship between the New York City Ballet and Saratoga Springs. This program is the brainchild of Dance Alliance president Mary Ann Fantauzzi and New York City Ballet dancers Justin Peck and Andrew Scordato. As a part of the Saratoga Dances project, New York City Ballet dancers participate in educational programs for area high school students and teach master classes at Skidmore College, the National Museum of Dance and local studios.[147]

Saratoga Dances debuted in the Skidmore College Dance Theater in 2011. It featured three New York City Ballet dancers in the world premier of *The Enormous Room*, choreographed by Justin Peck with costumes designed by Mr. Scordato.

The sold-out performance of Saratoga Dances II was held in the fall of 2012 at the Zankel Music Center on the Skidmore College campus. New

York City Ballet dancers performed in the world premier of *Yaddo Shadow*, a duet by Mr. Peck, and in George Balanchine's *Apollo*.[148] Debra Fernandez' *Swan Song* was performed by Skidmore dancers and two guests from the New York City Ballet.

Choreographer Justin Peck shared his thoughts on the *Saratoga Dances* project:

> *It was so rewarding to see that we had sold out the large Zankel venue; it made all our hard work worthwhile. Plus, the venue itself is so incredible; seeing the dancers with the glass backdrop overlooking the woods of Saratoga was both distinctive and remarkable. This made me want to continue to bring dance to the Saratoga Springs community during the NYCB off-season.*
>
> *It is great to present my work here. Saratoga may be a small town, but the people are passionate about dance. They are a real "dance crowd!" They respect the art form, and they have a genuine interest in it. Since they see a lot of dance, I can feel free to try out a slew of ideas on them. Saratoga Dances has been a great testing ground for me to develop certain concepts and movements. It has certainly aided in my development as a choreographer.*[149]

PARTNERS IN DANCE

The combined efforts of several organizations are often necessary in order for a dance company to visit the area. In 1991, dance advocate Toni Smith brought regional dance presenters together with Beverly D'Anne of the New York State Council on the Arts. They discussed forming a cooperative organization to support touring dance companies, either with direct financial assistance or in-kind services.

Partners in Dance: A Consortium of Capital Region Dance Sponsors enables dance companies to come to Saratoga Springs to perform, offer master classes and present educational dance programs in public schools. The organization aids in advertising in print, radio and television, produces a detailed dance calendar and shares resources such as artist housing and outreach activities.[150]

Local members of Partners in Dance include the Dance Alliance, Nacre, National Museum of Dance, Saratoga Savoy, Tango Fusion, Skidmore College Dance Department and Office of Special Programs. Several individuals who are involved in the performing arts are also participating members.

The following dance companies that have performed in Saratoga Springs have been supported in part by Partners in Dance: Pearson/Widrig Dance Company, Paul Taylor Dance Company, Taylor 2, Battleworks, Ellen Sinopoli Dance Company, José Limón Dance Company, Martha Graham Dance Company and Nacre. Several programs at the National Museum of Dance and Saratoga ArtsFest dance workshops have received funding and organizational assistance.[151]

Chapter 9

Arts Education at Saratoga Performing Arts Center with the New York City Ballet

Education Programs for Students

The Saratoga Performing Arts Center continues its commitment to bringing the best of the arts to the region's children:

> *Arts education has always been a primary concern for SPAC, which was conceived and incorporated as an educational institution. Education remains the broad base from which the Center builds. Once the debut season was behind it, SPAC immediately embarked on a series of ambitious educational projects designed to develop both future audiences and performers.*[152]

In the summer of 1967, the Saratoga Performing Arts Center initiated an educational program with three distinct schools, one of which was the Ballet School. The New York City Ballet administered the program, and its School of American Ballet provided the faculty. This program was the predecessor of the New York State Summer School of the Arts Schools of Ballet and Dance. The development of these successful state-funded dance programs illustrated the cooperative partnership among New York State and the Saratoga Performing Arts Center, Skidmore College and the National Museum of Dance, the primary dance education institutions of Saratoga Springs.

Beginning in the second season at the Saratoga Performing Arts Center, matinee performances of the ballet were scheduled for student groups.

Children's Workshop on the Lawn with a dancer from the New York City Ballet. *Photo by Richard Cohen, courtesy of the Saratoga Performing Arts Center.*

Saratoga Seminars was a related program for schoolteachers and dance educators, sponsored jointly by the Arts Center and the State University of New York. Students enjoyed meeting dancers and hearing firsthand about the performance. Teachers then continued the conversation back in the classroom.

In 1983, the Freihofer Baking Company began its program of sponsoring free lawn passes to the ballet for children. As a result, countless local children have grown up on the lawn of the Saratoga Performing Arts Center. Generations of parents have been grateful for the exposure to world-class performing arts as part of their children's education.

Herb Chesbrough, president of the Saratoga Performing Arts Center, commented, "Over time, we are confident that the fact that they've been here, understood and had fun, will bring them back at some point in their lives."[153]

The Children's Workshops on the Lawn are sponsored by the Albany Medical Center. New York City Ballet dancers offer lively participatory activities for young children and their families, giving them a chance to "dance" with the professionals.[154]

The Saratoga Performing Arts Center's efforts spread beyond the venue itself when, in 1993, it initiated an integrated arts education program in public schools. Class Action was a program that brought singers, dancers and musicians into the classrooms to introduce students in grades five through seven to classical music and ballet. Instructional materials were provided to the teachers, who created lesson plans around a particular work. A musician or dancer then visited the classroom, thus forming a personal connection between the students and performer. Finally, students and teachers attended a performance of the same work they studied, performed by the same artist they met. Students who completed this two-year program received a free lawn pass for every summer season through their junior year of high school.

This outstanding model arts education program has been sponsored by many local and regional companies, such as Time Warner Cable, CDPHP, the Freedom Forum, Taylor Made, Target, McGregor Links Foundation and Aramark. Now sponsored by Union College, Class Action was renamed Classical Kids in 2009.[155]

The Saratoga Performing Arts Center Action Council also provides support for educational outreach and audience enrichment. Since 2005, the Vivienne Anderson Children's Program gives underprivileged children the chance to visit the National Museum of Dance, meet a New York City Ballet dancer and see a matinee ballet performance. This program has introduced over 1,500 children to the performing arts, an opportunity many would otherwise not have had.[156]

Education Programs for Adults

Beginning in 1986, the National Museum of Dance sponsored free lectures and *Pre-Curtain Talks* for adults. Presented by trained museum docents and local dance professionals, audience members gained insight into that evening's dance program. The talks moved in 1990 from the museum to the gazebo on the Saratoga Performing Arts Center lawn and continued for several seasons. Antoinette (Toni) Smith, who was the director in the summer of 1990, said, "This is a learning museum rather than a fine arts museum. It is a dance museum, and dance is about movement, so we have to showcase this movement in everything we present."[157]

Saratoga Performing Arts Center educational programs have expanded to include several opportunities for adults on-site. In 2008, the informative presentations before the ballet performances returned.

The Pre-Performance Talks are ticketed events held near the Hall of Springs. This program boasts a roster of first-rate professional dancers, choreographers, dance writers and ballet conductors.

Past lectures have included: "NYCB 2000, Flexibility and Constancy" by ballet master in chief Peter Martins, "Dancing at the Speed of Balanchine" by former principal dancer Merrill Ashley and "Balanchine's Relationship with Stravinsky's Music" by ballet conductor Andrea Quinn. Well-known dance writer Deborah Jowitt presented "Games, Dreams and Dancing Like Fred Astaire: The Diverse Aspects of Jerome Robbins," and writer Mindy Aloff lectured on "Lincoln Kirstein's Taste in Art." Several local arts personalities have hosted and introduced these distinguished guests, including Skidmore professor emeritus Charles Joseph, an expert on Stravinsky and Jay Rogoff who writes on dance for the *Saratogian.* Former New York City Ballet dancers Robert Maiorano and brothers William and David Otto have hosted interviews with their colleagues.[158]

The New York City Ballet initiated the newest pre-performance experience in 2011. *See the Music* is a program that showcases the New York City Ballet orchestra and company's extensive musical repertoire. The conductor briefly discusses the musical selections in that evening's program, and the orchestra plays excerpts of the piece.[159] Former soloist David Otto remembers that George Balanchine frequently said, "You must hear the dance and see the music."[160]

DANCE ACTIVITIES AT SARATOGA SPRINGS HIGH SCHOOL

Mary Ann Fantauzzi is a Saratoga Springs High School mathematics teacher who works tirelessly to bring dance into her students' lives. Ms. Fantauzzi is a long-term docent for the National Museum of Dance, the president of the Dance Alliance and a loyal fan of the New York City Ballet. She is the owner of the local fitness studio Total Body Trifecta, where she has been teaching the "NYCB Workout" since 1997.[161] Through her annual training and re-certification, Ms. Fantauzzi has developed a close relationship with the New York City Ballet, which is advantageous to her ongoing efforts in dance education here in Saratoga Springs.

At the high school, Ms. Fantauzzi created a physical education dance elective course that incorporates the NYCB Workout into a comprehensive curriculum. Students gain a complete experience that combines lecture, video observation, creative work and movement participation. Ms. Fantauzzi's Saratoga Springs High School course is the only officially sanctioned NYCB

MOVE Dance Club at Saratoga Springs High School. *Photo provided by Mary Ann Fantauzzi.*

Workout program outside New York City, and it fulfills the mandated New York State dance curriculum for public schools. On video, students study samples of the company's repertoire and hear dancers speak about the works. Students then have the opportunity to create their own choreography inspired by the ballet they studied. They also do the NYCB Workout exercise program throughout the term. In addition to the course, all participants take a guided tour of the National Museum of Dance and receive free lawn tickets for a ballet performance at the Saratoga Performing Arts Center.

Mary Ann Fantauzzi also administers an after-school dance program in the high school. In 2001, the Dance Alliance's Youth Outreach program began and funded a dance group whose mission was to "accept and celebrate diversity through dance." Under the guidance of dancers from Skidmore College, students create and perform their own work. The group adopted the name MOVE and now is an officially sanctioned student club at the high school.

In addition to her regular dance activities, Ms. Fantauzzi recently brought two dancers from the New York City Ballet to speak in high school music and English classes. Andrew Scordato and Justin Peck discussed Stravinsky's *Firebird* with orchestra players, and they used scenes from Peter Martin's ballet *Romeo+Juliet* and Jerome Robbins's *West Side Story* in the English classes to illustrate themes from Shakespeare's play.[162]

Thanks to the Saratoga Performing Arts Center and the New York City Ballet, the students of Saratoga Springs have had the opportunity to learn directly from dancers and musicians who are at the top of their professions. The opportunity to attend performances free of charge encourages students to make the arts a meaningful part of their lives now and in the future.

Chapter 10
New York State Summer School of the Arts (NYSSSA)

The School of Ballet

The Saratoga Performing Arts Center had already established the city of Saratoga Springs as an exciting destination for those who love the arts. The success of the three training schools sponsored by the Saratoga Performing Arts Center, the New York City Ballet and the Philadelphia Orchestra had prepared the way for an expanded statewide arts education program.

In the late 1960s, Governor Nelson Rockefeller ordered the New York State Education Department to conduct a study on the status of the arts and humanities in New York. After the findings, the New York State legislature voted to support a summer arts education program for New York's gifted students. In 1970, the New York State Summer School of the Arts (NYSSSA) introduced the School of Orchestral Studies in Saratoga Springs. The school was directed by Maestro Eugene Ormandy, who chose a faculty of musicians from the Philadelphia Orchestra. Students were accepted by audition, regardless of ability to pay. The success of this school led to the 1976 addition of five new programs: the Schools of Media Arts, Choral Studies, Theatre, Visual Arts and Ballet.

To coincide with the summer residency of the New York City Ballet, the School of Ballet is also located in Saratoga Springs. The artistic directors and faculty of the School of Ballet are all dancers or teachers from the company. They deliver a curriculum that includes classes in ballet technique, pointe, men's technique, repertoire, character dance and pas de deux. Students perform a demonstration of their work at the end of the program.

The professional staff has complete control over the audition process. Auditions are held in three locations around New York: in Saratoga Springs, at the School of American Ballet in New York City and at SUNY Brockport. Each year, a group of thirty-five dancers, ages eleven to eighteen, is chosen. Students regularly attend ballet performances at the Saratoga Performing Arts Center, and many have the opportunity to perform with the New York City Ballet when the repertoire requires young dancers.

Melissa Hayden directed the pilot program, and Ricky Weiss was the first long-term director, assisted by Bojan Spassof. Subsequent directors have included Heather Watts and Damien Woetzel; Jenifer Ringer and Daniel Ulbricht currently direct the school. A master teacher from the School of American Ballet, Olga Kostritsky has been instrumental in building the program.

Prior to 1992, the School of Ballet utilized various locations around the city because the Skidmore College dance facilities were in use during July. Students were housed on campus, but they were bussed to Lake Avenue School, Spa Little Theatre and Skidmore's Moore Hall for classes. Open spaces in these buildings were adapted into studios with a state-of-the-art portable dance floor designed by New York City Ballet's production manager, Eddie Bigelow.[163]

THE SCHOOL OF DANCE

By the 1980s, dance fans were enjoying modern dance performances at the Spa Little Theatre and exploring the exhibits at Saratoga's newest gem, the National Museum of Dance.

The New York State legislature supplied funding to open two additional arts schools in 1988—the School of (Modern) Dance and the School of Jazz (Music). Saratoga Springs was the chosen location, due to the multitude of dance activities in the city and its proximity to Jacob's Pillow Dance Festival and Bennington College.

Carolyn Adams, a well-known dancer with the Paul Taylor Dance Company, was selected as artistic director. She had connections throughout the diverse modern dance world.

Carolyn Adams and her sister, Julie Adams Strandberg, had founded the American Dance Legacy Institute, a program that preserves the work of the pioneers of modern dance. They adapted this program's comprehensive college curriculum for the summer high school students. Some of the early choreographers who worked directly with students were Donald McKayle, Anna Sokolow, Mary Anthony and Daniel Nagrin.

The current curriculum also represents the work of contemporary choreographers. Students study dance techniques, repertory, composition and music for dance. The exhibits and programs at the National Museum of Dance are an integral part of the course, and students attend modern dance performances whenever possible. At the close of the session, students perform the repertory they have learned and their own original work in a final showcase at the Skidmore Dance Theater.

Contemporary teachers have included members of the Paul Taylor Dance Company, Robert Battle's Battleworks and the David Parsons Dance Company. Guest artists from visiting companies also offer master classes.

The School of Dance students and staff have been housed on the Skidmore College campus. For the first five years, all classes were held in the Skidmore dance studios that were available during the August program.

Groundbreaking for the Lewis A. Swyer School of the Arts, with Carolyn Adams, Heather Watts, Edward Swyer, Marylou Whitney and others. *Photo provided by the National Museum of Dance.*

In 1992, the New York State Summer School of the Arts Schools of Ballet and Modern Dance moved into the Lewis A. Swyer School of Dance, a state-of-the-art studio facility built behind the National Museum of Dance. They now had a home to call their own, where the programs could continue to offer students the best in ballet and modern dance training.[164]

> *The Mary Daley Scholarship has been created by past and present dance program participants to aid future artists as they pursue their training. This award honors the more than thirty years of dedicated service by Mary Daley, Executive Director Emerita of the New York State Summer School of the Arts.*[165]

Chapter 11

Dance Around the City

ArtsFest

The Saratoga ArtsFest was originally intended to be a vehicle for Skidmore to reach out and share cultural resources with the local community.[166] Marie Glotzbach, wife of Skidmore president Phil Glotzback, initiated the idea of bringing together local artists and arts organizations to facilitate the project.

Started in 2007, ArtsFest is now an annual four-day summer festival of local, regional and national performing and visual artists. The purchased ArtsPass enables the public to attend all events during the festival and to receive discounted admission to many cultural events throughout the year.[167]

From the beginning, both professional and local dance ensembles have been featured participants. Several of the major dance companies in residence at Skidmore College have opened the festivities with performance on campus or at the Saratoga Performing Arts Center. The festival's other dance performances have taken place at a wide variety of venues throughout the city, including the Spa Little Theatre, Skidmore College Dance Theater and Zankel Music Center, the National Museum of Dance, Universal Preservation Hall and even the East Side Recreation Field and the Saratoga Polo Fields.[168]

Choreographer Debra Fernandez has this to say about her participation in projects for Saratoga ArtsFest:

> *From this artist's point of view, ArtsFest has provided me with two wonderful opportunities to show my work in the Zankel Music Center. I think the Dance Department has benefitted from both the exposure and from the opportunity for our students to perform in such a professional setting. These performances connect us with larger audiences and enhance and expand the reputation of the department. Through ArtsFest, we also make connections with other professional dance artists who come to Saratoga Springs to participate.*[169]

The Saratoga ArtsFest has presented the following dance ensembles:

2007
Bill T. Jones/Arnie Zane Dance Company*
CoMotion in Motion
Lilly Loveday Dance Performance
Tango Fusion

2008
Dancing With Horses: The Equus Project
Debra Fernandez and Dancers
Ellen Sinopli Dance Company
Martha Graham Dance Company* with student workshop dancers
Wise Monkey Dance Company

2009
Company Stefanie Batten-Bland
Paul Taylor Dance Company*
Taylor 2* and students of Skidmore Summer Dance Showcase

2010
Ellen Sinopoli Dance Company
Gallim*
José Limón Dance Company*
Music and Motion,* choreography by Debra Fernandez and Rubén Graciani; Richard Danielpour, composer

2011
Ariel Rivka Dance
Lar Lubovich Dance Company*
Saratoga Dances I

2012

Bill T. Jones/Arnie Zane Dance Company with Anne Bogart's SITI Company*

DNA Works: *HaMapah*

Ellen Sinopoli Dance Company

Keeping Company with Cage,* choreography by Debra J. Fernandez; David Porter, piano

*dance company or event sponsored through Skidmore College Office of the Dean of Special Programs

Dance Flurry

The Dance Flurry came to town in 1988, presenting dozens of dance and music workshops in traditional folk and social dances. Contradance, English country, squares, clogging, Scandinavian and Chinese folk dance are just some of the forms offered. Every year, a large multigenerational group of enthusiastic dancers comes to Saratoga from far and wide for this weekend festival. The Dance Flurry events are held at the First Baptist Church, the Parting Glass, City Center, Hilton Garden Inn, Skidmore College and the Saratoga Music Hall.[170]

Street Festivals

There are two annual downtown celebrations that showcase a multitude of performers: the Victorian Streetwalk ushers in the holiday season, and First Night Saratoga celebrates New Year's Eve with a city-wide festival of the arts. Participating dancers, both students and professionals, perform at the Saratoga Music Hall, Universal Preservation Hall, National Museum of Dance, Skidmore Dance Theater and the Spa Little Theatre.

DANCE AT YADDO

Yaddo, the four-hundred-acre estate of Spencer and Katrina Trask, offers residencies to professional creative artists of all types. Through a highly competitive process, these prestigious awards enable artists to produce their work in a very private setting as they enjoy the peaceful surroundings of the estate.

Twyla Tharp and Christopher D'Amboise have both been in residence at Yaddo. However, opportunities for dance artists have been limited due to inadequate facilities on-site. Renovations are currently underway, and a new building is replacing the Greenhouse Studios. This new studio space with properly sprung floors opens the possibilities for more choreographers and performance artists at Yaddo.[171]

Yaddo has inspired artists, and many have honored the institution with their work. During its 2000 residency at Skidmore College, the Trisha Brown Dance Company presented performances commemorating the 100th anniversary of Yaddo. The 2012 Saratoga Dances II program reflected Yaddo's mission of supporting and bringing together artists of various disciplines. Choreographer Justin Peck debuted his duet *Yaddo Shadow*, danced by two members of the New York City Ballet.

SARATOGA RACE COURSE

Even the Thoroughbreds at the Saratoga Race Course are involved with dance in Saratoga. NYRA established the "Ballerina Stakes" in 1979. Named for the Thoroughbred Ballerina, this seven-furlong race is run during the last week of August as part of the Breeders' Cup.

In August 2012, NYRA debuted a new race, the "National Museum of Dance," also a seven-furlong race. Museum staff and board members cheered, and costumed dance students from the School of the Arts strolled among the crowds.[172]

EN POINTE!

As people stroll through Saratoga in the summers, they see painted and decorated horse sculptures placed around town. Soon there will be sculptures of a ballerina's foot on pointe, uniquely painted by local artists.

En Pointe! sculptures in progress. *Photo provided by the National Museum of Dance.*

This celebration of dance is a program initiated by the National Museum of Dance and is sponsored by many individuals and local businesses. The pointe shoe sculptures will be unveiled in summer 2013.

Chapter 12
The Dance Audience

Dance Fans of Saratoga

An audience often includes a variety of people who attend a performance for different reasons. Some are curious, some are simply enjoying a night out and some are avid fans of the performers. The Saratoga dance fans are a large, surprisingly diverse group of people who share a love of dance and a loyalty to the New York City Ballet. That common bond inspires them to come together to advocate for maintaining the company's residency at the Saratoga Performing Arts Center.

New York City Ballet's ballet master in chief Peter Martins has said of Saratoga's dance audience:

> *In sheer sophistication and knowledge, I think our Saratoga audiences are, by far, more educated and advanced in terms of judging ballets than most audiences in the world. By coming to the ballet for many years, you get an understanding of the ballet.*[173]

Mrs. Kay Leach has been a fan and supporter of the New York City Ballet's Saratoga seasons from the very beginning. Her husband, Richard Leach, was the first executive director of the Saratoga Performing Arts Center, and they were both intimately involved with the company. Mrs. Leach shared her memories of the ballet:

> *July was a dream. There were so many exalting moments—Suzanne was so wonderful; Patty was adorable and everyone loved her; Kay Mazzo was lovely. At certain times it was so extraordinary, it would make you dizzy. It could hit you so.*[174]

The Saratoga dance fans are aware of a select group among them who are referred to as the "every nighters." For these fans, attending the ballet nightly is, without question, the natural thing to do. For other fans, it is something to aspire to.

Sheila Parkert, former owner of the Adelphi Hotel, admits, "I have always been a huge ballet fan, an every nighter!"[175] "Of course I'm an every nighter," says Mary Ann Fantauzzi.[176] Christie Handley, a former dancer who now teaches ballet, remembers, "My first summer, I went to SPAC every show for four weeks, matinee and evening."[177] Rhona Kretzky-Forman states, "Those ballet weeks are sacred to me. I have a group of friends who are fans, and we are all working towards becoming every nighters."[178]

Several dedicated ballet fans began working for the Saratoga Performing Arts Center or with the New York City Ballet in one capacity or another. Their love of the ballet, their awe of George Balanchine and their pride in having this company in their midst compelled each of them to participate in the ballet experience. They have been among the most determined advocates for protecting the New York City Ballet's residency at the Saratoga Performing Arts Center.

Mary Ann Fantauzzi is the indefatigable liaison between the New York City Ballet and the people of Saratoga Springs. She is a Saratoga Springs High School mathematics teacher who also owns a fitness studio where she teaches the NYCB Workout program.[179] Through her annual certification in the program, she has a working relationship with the New York City Ballet.

Ms. Fantauzzi is one of the founding writers for Saratoga's summer dance newsletter, *Ballet Beat*. She is also an original member of two local organizations, For Arts Sake and Save the Ballet. Her work with the Dance Alliance, of which she is president, has resulted in the successful Saratoga Dances I and II projects. These multifaceted projects showcase the work of the young choreographer Justin Peck and the emerging ballet teacher and costume designer Andrew Scordato. With great pride, Mary Ann Fantauzzi refers to these talented young artists as "my boys."[180]

As a teenage ballet student, Christie Handley came to Saratoga to study in the summer with Melissa Hayden. Many New York City Ballet company dancers attended Ms. Hayden's classes while they were in town. Ms. Handley

Mary Ann Fantauzzi and Justin Peck, dancer and choreographer at the New York City Ballet. *Photo by Anthony Tassarotti.*

went to the Saratoga Performing Arts Center for every performance, "frequently sneaking in backstage like one of the dancers so I could watch from the wings. I saw it all—I even met Mr. Balanchine!"

Ms. Handley enrolled part time in Skidmore College to continue her training with Melissa Hayden and then with Elisabeth Carroll and Michael Steele. After sustaining an injury, Ms. Handley began teaching ballet for Ballet Regent and other area schools. She studied costume design in New York City and immediately began sewing costumes for Ms. Carroll's student performances at Skidmore College.

At the age of twenty, Ms. Handley started her summer job backstage with the New York City Ballet. She was initially hired as a dresser for the children, but she moved to the corps de ballet room and soon on to the soloists. She was eventually assigned to work with the principal dancers, dressing Suzanne Farrell, Darci Kistler, Wendy Whelan, Sara Mearns and others.

Year round, Christie Handley continues to share her passionate love of ballet with her students at the National Museum of Dance School of the Arts. During the July ballet season, she is dedicated to her work as a principal dresser for the New York City Ballet, and she is still there to see every performance. "How could I not be a ballerina and still have had all these wonderful opportunities and experiences at such a high level—Saratoga IS ballet land!"[181]

Rhona Koretzky-Forman came to Saratoga in 1978. Having started ballet in college, she continued in adult classes with Michael Steele. "I believe the more you study, the more respect you develop for the art form." She recalls the first time she attended a performance of the New York City Ballet at the Saratoga Performing Arts Center: "The program included Balanchine's *In G Major*.[182] I had no idea what a cornerstone of my life the New York City Ballet presence would become."

This initial summer ballet experience compelled her to become a volunteer usher for the Saratoga Performing Arts Center at a time when ushers received guest passes for performances. Ms. Koretzky-Forman was soon employed as usher captain and was responsible for educating the ushers and house staff: "It was a wonderful thing to be a part of, a real privilege to be a small cog in this incredible machinery."

She was thrilled to be sharing her hometown in the summers with the company, especially with George Balanchine: "Here in Saratoga Springs, we were intersecting with Genius." Ms. Koretzky-Forman believes that some of the sense of tradition from that time has been lost: "The loss of Balanchine left a chasm, but we still had Maestro Ormandy and Jerome Robbins. I can still, even to this day, feel Balanchine's presence at SPAC. That was Balanchine's house."

Ms. Koretzky–Forman also enjoyed seeing the modern dance companies at the Spa Little Theatre: "The modern dance festivals were incredible! I support having all styles of first-rate dance here."

As a city librarian, she worked to encourage and support arts education in public schools. She was one of the originators of the newsletter *Ballet Beat* and the organizations Save the Ballet and For Art's Sake. She has been a vocal advocate for keeping the New York City Ballet summer season at the Saratoga Performing Arts Center.[183]

Sue Edwards's life as a dedicated dance fan began when she was eighteen years old. During the first summer season of the Saratoga Performing Arts Center, she worked at a snack bar located in the Hall of Springs. The New York City Ballet dancers frequently stopped by, especially a young Suzanne Farrell, who became a good friend of Ms. Edwards. Volunteers and workers were invited to watch rehearsals and received free lawn passes to the performances.

Susan Edwards remembers seeing *Swan Lake* with Suzanne Farrell: "Her presence brought tears to my eyes every time, especially *Swan Lake*, which is and always will be the ballet I love the most."

Illustration from *Ballet Beat. Apollo* by Shawn Banner. Drawing inspired by *Apollo* choreography by George Balanchine. ©*The George Balanchine Trust.*

She goes to as many ballet performances as she can every season and has happy memories of that first summer when she met her now longtime friend Suzanne Farrell.

Although she enjoys and appreciates the Saratoga Performing Arts Center, Sue Edwards's primary dance interest is the National Museum of Dance. A constant volunteer since the earliest days of the museum, she is currently employed as the program director for the National Museum of Dance.[184]

The Saratoga Performing Arts Center requires the assistance of hundreds of volunteers who work as ushers, greeters and office help throughout the year. The program for the 1991 summer season features an article on a few of the many people who help keep the Arts Center going. These volunteers share a gratitude for the artists and take great pride in being a part of it all: the ballet, the orchestra, the opera and the popular programming. An unnamed volunteer is quoted as saying, "SPAC has the power to put beauty in your life. When you walk onto the grounds, you get this feeling that beauty is going to be there."[185]

The administration of the Saratoga Performing Arts Center expressed its gratitude in this statement:

> *Regardless of how much the volunteers feel SPAC has given to them, The Center is much in debt to each and every person who gives of themselves to contribute to the success and smooth running of SPAC. The time and enthusiasm that every volunteer contributes to the Center is an invaluable resource without which SPAC could not survive. We are indebted to their year-round time, spirit and cooperation.*[186]

There are others in Saratoga Springs who were never dancers themselves but were influential in supporting dance and bringing it to our area. Donald McCormack has been an energetic and determined advocate for dance in our community since the 1980s, when he took over as dean of special programs at Skidmore College. He championed modern dance and believed it deserved a dynamic presence in Saratoga Springs, complementing that of the New York City Ballet. "I believe we can really set the stage for great things happening." He was instrumental in organizing the Spa Little Theatre modern dance festivals starting in the 1980s and advocated for several modern dance companies to be showcased in the main stage of the amphitheater.

Now retired from Skidmore College, Donald McCormack continues having an impact on the cultural life of Saratoga Springs. He is a member of the board of directors of the Saratoga Performing Arts Center and is among the originators of the Extended Season/Emerging Artists series.[187]

Originally from New York City, Jay Rogoff is a poet, dance writer and avid ballet fan. His introduction to ballet was in high school, and he found himself "being drawn magnetically to the more abstract NYCB works, especially those by Balanchine and Robbins."

In 1985, Rogoff moved to Saratoga Springs to join the English Department at Skidmore College. He explained how his love of dance influenced his writing:

> *I came to dance writing at first through poetry. I wanted to capture the peculiar symbolic mental and emotional realm we enter when we watch*

> *ballet or modern dance, and I wanted to pay homage to the creators of dance who have meant so much to me. But I also wanted to integrate my appreciation of dance with the interactions in our daily lives between the ordinary and the extraordinary.*

Jay Rogoff wrote dance criticism for several publications prior to stepping in to write on the New York City Ballet seasons for the *Saratogian*:

> *The conflict between criticism and advocacy is especially germane to writing for the* Saratogian. *It's the hometown paper, and therefore I see part of my job as advertising what is so good about NYCB, since I think it's so important that they stay at SPAC. In the paper I'm writing for a general audience who, I hope, is interested in finding out why ballet is worthwhile, why it might be something they'd like to try attending, and I want to encourage them that, yes, this is a really exciting kind of entertainment that we don't have to be afraid of, that can provide an enjoyable evening out, and at its best can even admit us into the sublime.*[188]

Jay Rogoff is the author of four books, including his most recent collection of dance-inspired poetry, *The Art of Gravity*. He also writes on dance for the *Hopkins Review* and the *Ballet Review*.[189]

Michele and Ronald Riggi are among Saratoga Springs' most prominent patrons of the ballet. Mrs. Riggi, a former dancer, has dedicated her energies to her position as the president of the National Museum of Dance. Ronald Riggi now sits on the board of directors of the Saratoga Performing Arts Center, and he brings his knowledge of the community and business expertise to the table. Mr. Riggi believes that the relationship between the New York City Ballet and the Saratoga Performing Arts Center is solid. He states:

> *I am having a lot of fun with this. I enjoy being with community leaders and diverse professional people who share the same goal. The board has a great balance, and the administration and staff are all very dedicated. We believe SPAC and NYCB are synonymous, and both parties are very engaged. SPAC must tweak every revenue source, and NYCB must make sure they can get here. SPAC is a jewel in our hometown, and Saratoga and the region have to support it.*[190]

THE DANCE FANS ORGANIZE

There have been several grass-roots efforts to "save" the summer residency of the New York City Ballet at the Saratoga Performing Arts Center and to restore a four-week season. Two organizations have come together for this purpose.

For Arts Sake was started in 1998 by Mae Banner and a small group of locals who loved the ballet and the arts. In addition to advocating for the New York City Ballet residency, this group was determined to educate and inform the public. At Mae Banner's suggestion, it founded the summer dance publication *Ballet Beat*, a newsletter that celebrates the ballet season with articles about repertoire, choreographers, composers and the dancers.

Dance enthusiasts Mary Ann Fantauzzi, Rhona Koretzky-Forman, Alisa Forman and Jay Rogoff are contributing writers for *Ballet Beat*. Artist Shawn Banner provides illustrations, and typeset and layout are donated by Paul Chessare. This volunteer publication is jointly funded by the Lyrical Ballad Bookstore, Total Body Trifecta Fitness Studio and the National Museum of Dance. *Ballet Beat* is dedicated to the memory of Mae G. Banner.[191]

Save the Ballet has been in existence since 2004, when the entire summer ballet season was in jeopardy of being cancelled. This growing group of determined fans has worked tirelessly to communicate their mission of ensuring that the New York City Ballet remains in residence at the Saratoga Performing Arts Center. Many ideas have been discussed, generated by dance lovers who desperately want to save something they know is important to them and to Saratoga Springs.

Countless people have voiced their opinions, but two particular local citizens have distinguished themselves by their words and deeds: former mayor of Saratoga Springs Raymond Watkin and the late Mae G. Banner.

Mayor Raymond Watkin has always known that Saratoga Springs is a dance town. Before the days of the Saratoga Performing Arts Center, he sold ballet and tap shoes at his Broadway shoe store, Raymond's Bootery. He befriended and supported the city's dance teachers and dance personalities. Watkin's business funded an annual scholarship for local dance students to continue their training in Saratoga Springs.

Mayor Watkin understood the impact the Saratoga Performing Arts Center had on the entire region. In the 1970s, he publicly celebrated the New York City Ballet, and he fought against shortening the four-week season.

Now retired, the walls of his home are covered with dance posters and memorabilia from his days as a mayor who loved and supported the New

York City Ballet in his town. Mayor Raymond Watkin declared recently, "We owe allegiance to New York City Ballet. People in Saratoga need to voice outrage at the current state of affairs, and we need to fight for this! The people should not be afraid to speak up."[192]

No one in Saratoga Springs has done more to support dance, to educate the public and to advocate for dance than Mae Banner. Ms. Banner came to Saratoga Springs in 1977 as a new faculty member at Skidmore College. She immediately began ushering, along with other schoolteachers and die-hard dance fans, at the Saratoga Performing Arts Center while her young son Shawn played on the lawn.

After leaving Skidmore, Mae Banner chose to remain in Saratoga and started writing for the *Saratogian* and *Metroland.* She insisted that the newspapers make space for dance reviews and articles, saying, "This is important, and we must include it. I want people to know how it feels—I want to put them in it."

According to Shawn Banner, "Mae lived and breathed dance, learning as she went and spending time with all the serious dance fans. She was a good friend of local celebrities Zachary Solov and John Martin, who educated her eye for dance and helped her with proper dance terminology." She wrote about ballet and modern dance at the Saratoga Performing Arts Center, the Spa Little Theatre, the Egg, Jacob's Pillow Dance Festival and the Kaatsbaan International Dance Centre. Ms. Banner also spoke on WAMC and served on state and local arts panels.

Mae Banner's first love was the "dance from the gut" of the modern dance pioneers, and she especially loved the work of Paul Taylor and Garth Fagan. She was a staunch supporter of the New York State Summer School of the Arts School of Dance and of Carolyn Adams's and Julie Adams Strindberg's work with the American Dance Legacy Institute. The Banner Award was established to honor the efforts of the hardest-working student in the annual Summer School of Dance.

Although Mae Banner was never a trained dancer, she was able to understand the intent of the dances. Shawn Banner explained:

> *While watching her favorite ballets, she would catch her breath and hold it-feeling the thrill of the moment. She never tired of seeing ballets again and again, and she relished observing multiple casts in the same works. Among her favorites were Balanchine's* Serenade *and Robbins's* Dances at a Gathering, *and dancers Kyra Nichols and Bart Cook made her heart flutter.*

She was a true fan who absolutely believed that the Saratoga Performing Arts Center was meant to enrich the community through high art, not popular entertainment.[193]

In July 2007, the New York City Ballet and Saratoga Performing Arts Center honored Mae Banner, dedicating a performance of Balanchine's *Jewels* to her memory and naming her favorite seat in row W with an engraved plaque. Before that evening's performance, first Marcia White and then Peter Martins paid tribute to Mae, speaking to the audience from the stage:

Illustration from *Ballet Beat. Serenade* by Shawn Banner. Drawing inspired by *Serenade* choreography by George Balanchine. ©*The George Balanchine Trust.*

> *Mae Banner was a true champion of the arts. As a writer and dance reviewer for the* Saratogian, *Mae believed very strongly that the critic's role was one of both educator and advocate. Her articles inspired readers to take full advantage of this area's rich cultural offerings and to open themselves to new artistic experiences.*
>
> *This tribute to Mae is a great opportunity to honor a woman who not only loved dance, but understood its importance as an art form. Mae had a remarkable ability in her reviews to interpret and describe the ballets with such richness and meaning, that it made even those of us in the company want to see the dance again through Mae's unique lens. She will be greatly missed both personally and professionally, yet her contribution to dance and the arts community will continue to have an impact.*[194]

Mae Banner's son Shawn grew up with his mother's love of dance, music and language, which she passed on to her grandchildren. When they accompanied her to performances, she would ask the children for their responses and frequently used their words in her reviews and articles. Shawn Banner honors his mother's legacy and tries to continue some of her work. He knows he is Saratoga's connection back to Mae and that the people of Saratoga Springs loved her.

Appendix 1

Skidmore College Department of Dance Faculty and Staff

Tenured Faculty

Debra J. Fernandez, Professor and Chair of Dance
Denise Warner Limoli, Associate Professor
Mary DiSanto-Rose, Associate Professor
Rubén Graciani, Associate Professor

Mary Harney, Artist in Residence

Lecturers

Antoinette Smith
David Otto
Debra Pigliavento
Julie Gedalecia
Megan Del Prete
Sarah DiPasquale
Veena Chandra

Dance Musicians

Carl Landa, Director of Music
Carol Ann Elze Sussdorf
Patricia Hadfield

Skidmore Dance Theater

Lori Dawson, Technical Director, Lighting Designer, Manager
Peter Kobor, Assistant to the Technical Director and Stage Manager

Debra Nichols, Administrative Assistant

Appendix 2
Skidmore College Dance Faculty Biographies

Debra J. Fernandez, Professor

Debra Fernandez is a director/choreographer and dance educator. She is classically trained, self-taught in jazz and has a sustaining interest in experimental theater.

In 1990, she joined the dance faculty at Skidmore College, where she began teaching Ballet III, Contemporary Workshop, Choreography I and II and Performance Elements.

She was invited to join the Williamstown Theater Festival in 1994 and remained a member for seven years. While there, she worked with several influential directors, especially director Phil Soltanoff. In 1999, she was choreographer for the Virginia Opera's production of *Orfeo and Euridice* directed by Darko Tresjnak. Her collaboration with director David Pilot and composer Joseph Diebes, *The Malleus Maleficarum*, was presented at the Ontological Theater in New York.

In 2000, the Tang Museum and Art Gallery opened at Skidmore College, and Debra established a close and lasting relationship with the museum. Since its opening, she has made four evening-length works that have allowed her to focus on the museum as an interactive performance space: *TangO*, *BALLS*, *MAK 3* and *Zero Point Zero.*

In the Arthur Zankel Music Center, Debra choreographed *Swan Song* to a score by Richard Danielpour in 2010 and *Keeping Company with Cage*, her third collaboration with David Porter and Margo Mensing, in 2012.

Debra has received choreography fellowships to the Djerassi Resident Center for the Arts in California and the Wurlitzer Foundation in Taos, New Mexico. She has served on the New York State Council for the Arts and the New York State Foundation for the Arts and as chair of the scholarship committee for the Saratoga City Ballet.

DENISE WARNER LIMOLI, ASSOCIATE PROFESSOR

Denise Warner Limoli trained in Connecticut with Mme. Vera Nikitins of the Riga Opera Ballet. With a full scholarship, she attended both the Washington School of Ballet and, for three summers, Jacob's Pillow Dance Festival. In addition to classical ballet, her training included Graham and Limón modern dance, Bharatanatyam, Flamenco and character dance. She frequently studied in New York City at the Ballet Theatre School with the great teachers Valentina Pereyaslavec, Leon Danielian, Patricia Wilde and Yurek Lazowsky.

Ms. Warner Limoli performed with the Hartford Ballet, the Connecticut Opera and the Norfolk Civic Ballet before moving to New York City in 1970. She immediately began performing with the American Ballet Theatre (ABT) as a seasonal dancer and joined the company in 1972. With ABT, Ms. Warner Limoli performed all the great romantic and classical ballets, works of Tudor, MacMillan, Ashton, Robbins, Feld and others. She shared the Metropolitan Opera House stage and toured internationally with the greatest dancers of the day, such as Natalia Makarova, Cynthia Gregory, Mikhail Baryshnikov and Fernando Bujones. She taught company class regularly and was a substitute teacher in the Ballet Theatre School. She appeared in many PBS *Live from Lincoln Center* broadcasts and danced in the films *The Turning Point* and *First Position*.

After retiring from performing, Ms. Warner Limoli was ballet master for the Nutmeg Ballet Company, the Minnesota Dance Theatre and the Nevada Dance Theatre. She was a faculty member of the University of Cincinnati College-Conservatory of Music Dance Division and the North Carolina School of the Arts.

Denise Warner Limoli joined the Skidmore College dance faculty in 1992. She has worked to develop the curriculum and increase the rigor of the ballet program and has staged classical ballets and choreographed contemporary works for the Skidmore Ballet Workshop.

In 2011, Professor Limoli collaborated with the conductor of the Skidmore Orchestra, Professor Anthony Holland, on a joint production of *Swan Lake, Act II* in the Zankel Music Center. In 2013, Skidmore dancers and the Skidmore Orchestra presented An Evening with the Ballets Russes, including *Les Sylphides*, *L'Après Midi d'un Faune* and *Firebird*.

Ms. Warner Limoli has taught for the ABT Summer Intensives, the Kaatsbaan International Dance Center Extreme Ballet and the Nutmeg Conservatory International Summer Intensive. Locally, she has taught master classes and staged ballets for the Saratoga City Ballet and Ballet Regent. She is a member of the board of directors of the National Museum of Dance and is chair of the nominating committee for the Hall of Fame. She curated the exhibit "American Ballet Theatre: Then and Now" for the museum.

Denise Warner Limoli is married to Michael Limoli, renowned clarinetist and dance pianist. They have worked together in the ballet studio for over thirty years.

MARY DISANTO-ROSE, ASSOCIATE PROFESSOR

Mary DiSanto-Rose earned her MEd and EdD in dance from Temple University. She joined the Skidmore faculty in 1981 and served as director of the dance program from 1990 to 2005 and as chair of the newly formed Department of Dance from 2005 to 2009. She has taught modern dance technique, dance history, improvisation, modern dance Reconstruction Workshop, Dance for the Child, Senior Dance Capstone and a first-year Scribner Seminar. Earlier in her career, she performed with the Sybil Dance Company of Philadelphia and with Albany-area dance companies.

Mary specializes in reconstructing classic modern dance works of the early twentieth century. She currently co-directs and performs as a guest artist with the Isadora Duncan International Institute Dancers of New York City.

Mary has been an active board member of the Capital/Saratoga Dance Alliance for almost three decades and the co-coordinator of the Dance+ Festival for the past twenty-two years. She serves on the boards of Partners in Dance: A Consortium of Capital Region Dance Sponsors; NYS Dance Educators Association; and the NYS Council on the Arts Dance Panel.

Professor DiSanto-Rose is recipient of the Honorary Certificate in Isadora Duncan Studies from IDII in 2005; the Exceptional Service and Scholarship from the National Dance Association in 2007; the Innovative Leadership in Dance Education & Legacy from the American Dance Legacy Institute at Brown University in 2008; and an honorary degree, doctor of arts, in 2012 from St. Lawrence University.

RUBÉN GRACIANI, ASSOCIATE PROFESSOR

Rubén Graciani graduated from the North Carolina School of the Arts, where he majored in modern dance. After receiving his high school degree, Mr. Graciani was awarded a scholarship to attend the Juilliard School in New York City, where he also studied on scholarship with several major New York dance companies, including the Martha Graham Company and the Merce Cunningham Dance Company. Rubén completed his studies at the State University of New York–Purchase, receiving a bachelor of fine arts in dance. While attending Purchase, he was invited to perform in three International Festivals of Dance staged in Taiwan and China. He joined the Kevin Wynn Collection, a New York–based modern dance company while still a student at Purchase. After graduation, Rubén was invited to join the Mark Morris Dance Group. His five-year affiliation with the company resulted in national and international tours. Additionally, he has been a member of bopi's black sheep/dances by kraig patterson since its inception. Rubén received his MFA from the University of Maryland–College Park, where he presented nine works of choreography for the Maryland Dance Ensemble. In September 2005, he joined the faculty at Ohio University as an assistant professor. In addition to his work at Ohio University, Rubén has been a member of the Joe Goode Performance Group for two seasons, as well as a guest artist with the Brian Brooks Moving Company and sbb-thegroup, a Paris-based modern dance company. He has recently launched his own dance company, RG DanceProject.

MARY HARNEY, ARTIST IN RESIDENCE

Mary Harney joined the Skidmore dance faculty in 2000. During her tenure at Skidmore, she has taught all levels of modern dance technique, Modern Performance Workshop, Ballet I, Choreography I, the Dance Experience and Senior Dance Capstone.

Classically trained in upstate New York, Mary graduated with a BFA from SUNY Purchase College Conservatory of Dance. While at Purchase, she performed the works of many top choreographers. During this period, she also danced with the Martha Graham Dance Company.

Prior to her work at Skidmore, Mary served as a member of the dance faculty at Union College and the New York State Summer School of the Arts.

In the spring of 2012, Mary directed Skidmore modern dance students who were invited by Janet Eilber, artistic director of the Martha Graham Dance Company, to participate in the first annual University Partners Showcase in New York City. The Skidmore dancers performed Martha Graham's "Steps in the Street" from Martha Graham's *Chronicle* at the Joyce Theater.

Mary serves on the board of directors of the Capital Region Dance Alliance and is a site coordinator for the yearly Dance+ Festival at the National Museum of Dance. She is a member of the scholarship committees of both the Dance Alliance and the Saratoga City Ballet.

Appendix 3

Skidmore College Department of Dance Guest Artists in Ballet (Partial List)

Dwight Rhoden, Alvin Ailey American Dance Company, Complexions
John Meehan, American Ballet Theatre, Vassar College
Lorin Johnson, American Ballet Theatre, CalState/Long Beach
Martine Van Hamel, American Ballet Theatre
Steven Hyde, American Ballet Theatre
Susan Jones, American Ballet Theatre
Gina Bugati, Ballet Hispanico
Dariusz Hochman, Cannes, New York City
Abi Stafford, New York City Ballet
Alexandre Proia, Paris Opera, New York City Ballet
Andrew Scordato, New York City Ballet
David Otto, New York City Ballet
Justin Peck, New York City Ballet
Miranda Weese, New York City Ballet
Violette Verdy, New York City Ballet
William Otto, New York City Ballet
Alexei Tchernichov, Kirov Academy, Nutmeg Conservatory
Sharon Dante, Nutmeg Conservatory
Victoria Mazzarelli, Frankfurt Ballet, Nutmeg Conservatory
Kirsten Simone, Royal Danish Ballet
Summer Lee Rhatigan, San Francisco Conservatory of the Arts

Appendix 4

Saratoga Performing Arts Center Staff

Staff (Partial List)

Marcia White, President and Executive Director
Sharon Walsh, Assistant to the President/Director of Artistic Administration
Siobhan Dunham, Director Arts Education
Linda Deschenes, Director Youth Arts Programs
Lisa Hill, Public Relations/Development

Saratoga Performing Arts Center Board of Directors, Officers

Mrs. Marylou Whitney, Honorary Chair
Hon. Susan Read, Chair
Marcia White, President and Executive Director
Edward Lewy, Secretary
John Nigro, Treasurer

Appendix 5

New York City Ballet Staff

Artistic Staff

Founders: George Balanchine and Lincoln Kirstein
Founding Choreographers: George Balanchine and Jerome Robbins
Ballet Master in Chief: Peter Martins
Ballet Mistress: Rosemary Dunleavy
Ballet Masters: Karin von Aroldingen, Albert Evans, Jean-Pierre Frohlich, Susan Hendl, Glenn Keenan, Lisa Jackson, Sara Leland, Christine Redpath, Richard Tanner, Kathleen Tracey
Guest Teachers: Arch Higgins, Darci Kistler, Andrei Kramarevsky
Children's Ballet Master: Dena Abergel
Assistant Children's Ballet Master: Kaitlyn Gilliland
Personal Assistant to Mr. Martins: Deborah Koolish
Administrative Assistant to Mr. Martins: Julianne Maeda

The George Balanchine Trust

Director: Ellen Sorrin
Managing Trustee: Barbara Horgan
Coordinator: Nicole Cornell

Appendix 6

Repertoire Performed by the New York City Ballet at the Saratoga Performing Arts Center

1966–2012, Partial List

Choreography by George Balanchine, ©The George Balanchine Trust

Agon
Allegro Brilliante
Apollo
Baiser de la Fée
Ballet Imperial
Ballo della Regina
Brahms Quartet
Chaconne
Con Amore
Concerto Barocco
Coppélia
Cortège Hongrois
Duo Concertante
Firebird
Four Temperaments
Harlequinade
Irish Fantasy
Ivesiana
Jewels

La Sonnambula
La Valse
Le Bourgeois Gentilhomme
A Midsummer Night's Dream
Mozartiana
Nutcracker
Orpheus
Prodigal Son
Raymonda Variations
Scotch Symphony
Serenade
Slaughter on 10th Ave.
Square Dance
Stars and Stripes
Steadfast Tin Soldier
Stravinsky Violin Concerto
Suite No. 3
Swan Lake
Symphony in C (School of American Ballet)
Symphony in 3 Movements
Tarantella
Tchaikovsky Pas de Deux
Tchaikovsky Suite No. 2
Theme and Variations
Trois Valses Romantiques
Union Jack
Variations
Vienna Waltzes
Walpurgisnacht
Western Symphony
Who Cares?

Choreography by Jerome Robbins

2 and 3 Part Inventions
Afternoon of a Faun
Antique Epigraphs
Brahms/Handel (w/ Twyla Tharp)

Brandenburg
Bugaku
Circus Polka
Dances at a Gathering
Dybbuk Variations
Eight Lines
Fancy Free
Fanfare
Four Seasons
Glass Pieces
Goldberg Variations

In G Major
In Memory of…
Interplay
In the Night
Ives Songs
Les Noces
Other Dances
Piano Pieces
The Concert
West Side Story Suite

Choreography by Peter Martins

A Musical Offering
Ash
Beethoven Romance
Calcium Night Light
Capriccio Italien
Concerto for 2 Solo Pianos
Ecstatic Orange
Eight Easy Pieces
Eight Miniatures
Eight More
Fearful Symmetries

Four Gnossiennes
Guide to Strange Planets
Jeu de Cartes
Lille Suite
Poulenc Sonata
Romeo+Juliet
Sleeping Beauty
Sophisticated Lady
Swan Lake
Symphony No. 1
Tanzpiel
Tea Rose
Thou Swell
Valse Triste
Zakouski

Choreography by Christopher Wheeldon

After the Rain
American in Paris
Carnival of the Animals
DGV: Danse à Grande Vitesse
Estancia
Liturgy
Morphoses
Polyphonia
Rococo Variations

Choreography by Alexei Ratmansky

Concerto DSCH
Namouna, A Grand Divertissement
Russian Seasons

Appendix 6

Choreography by Twyla Tharp

Brahms/Handel (w/ Jerome Robbins)
The Beethoven Seventh

Also ballets by Anthony Tudor, Sir Frederic Ashton, John Taras, Merce Cunningham, Edward Villella, Richard Tanner, Stanley Williams, Benjamin Millepied, Justin Peck and other choreographers.

Appendix 7

Local Dance Schools and Directors

American Dance Center, Phyllis Latin; www.americandancecentersaratoga.com
Arthur Murray Dance Studio, Safwat Gerges; www.dancelessonssaratogasprings.com
Briansky Ballet Center, Oleg Briansky; www.briansky.org
The Dance Factory, Dianne Carola; www.dancefactorysaratoga.com
Myers Dance Center, Darlene Myers; www.myersnortheast.org
Nacre Dance Company, Beth Fecteau; www.nacredance.com
Saratoga Ballet Academy, David Otto; www.saratogaballetacademy.com
Saratoga City Ballet, Julie Gedalecia, Eve Welchel; www.saratogacityballet.com
Saratoga Savoy, Keira Lemonis, David F. Wolf; www.saratogasavoy.com
School of the Arts, Raul Martinez; www.dancemuseum.org/school
Stepping Star Gymnastics and Dance, Peggy Delay; www.steppingstar.com
Tango Fusion, Diane Lachtrupp, Johnny Martinez; www.tangofusiondance.com

Appendix 8

National Museum of Dance Staff

Staff (Partial List)

Director: Donna Skiff
Assistant Director: Sarah Hall Weaver
Design and Development: Ruby Whitney
Programming: Susan Edwards
Director, School of the Arts: Raul Martinez

National Museum of Dance Board of Directors, Officers

Founders: Mr. and Mrs. Cornelius Vanderbilt Whitney
Mr. Lewis Swyer
Honorary: Nancy Norman Lassalle
President: Michele Riggi
Secretary: Leslie Anne LaGuardia
Treasurer: John R. Aldrich, Esq.

Appendix 9

Skidmore College, Office of the Dean of Special Programs Staff

Summer Dance Program Staff

Paul Calhoun, Interim Dean of Special Programs (2011–)
Jeffrey Segrave, Dean of Special Programs (2006–2011)
Paula Newberg, Dean of Special Programs (2005–2006)
Donald McCormack, Dean of Special Programs (1986–2005)
Sharon Arpey, Director of Institutes, Conferences and Summer Operations
Maria McColl, Assistant Director of Institutes and Programs
Antoinette (Toni) Smith, Dance Faculty Advisor
Marianne Needham, Administrative Assistant

Appendix 10

Skidmore College Department of Dance and Office of the Dean of Special Programs

Modern Dance Guest Artists and Companies in Residence

Bebe Miller Dance Company
Bill T. Jones/Arnie Zane Dance Company
Brian Brooks, Brian Brooks Moving Company
Camille A. Brown, Camille A. Brown & Dancers
Company Stefanie Batten Bland
Dance by Neil Greenberg
Dan Wagoner Dance Company
David Dorfman Dance Company
David Gordon's Pick-Up Company
Deborah Hay, Performance Artist, Judson Church
Doug Varone & Dancers
Ellen Sinopoli, Sinopoli Dance Company
Erica Pujic, dancer Battleworks
Gallim Dance
Garth Fagan Dance
Hanna van der Kolk
José Limón Dance Company
Kevin Wynn, SUNY Purchase
Kraig Patterson, Mark Morris Dance Group
Lar Lubovich Dance Company
Mark Morris Dance Group

Martha Graham Dance Company
Parsons Dance Company
Paul Taylor Dance Company
Pearson/Widrig Dance Theater
Peter Pucci, Peter Pucci Plus Dancers
Randy James
Robert Battle, Artistic Director Alvin Ailey American Dance Company
Ronald K. Brown\Evidence
Shapiro & Smith Dance
Sydney Skybetter and Associates
Také
Taylor 2
Trisha Brown Dance Company
Twyla Tharp & Dancers

Appendix 11

Dance Organizations, Dance Departments, Dance Supplies

Dance Alliance, www.dancealliance.org
National Museum of Dance, www.dancemuseum.org
New York City Ballet, www.nycballet.com
New York State Summer School of the Arts (NYSSSA), www.oce.nysed.gov/nysssa
Saratoga Dance (dance supplies), www.saratogadance.com
Saratoga Performing Arts Center (SPAC), www.spac.org
Skidmore College Dance Department, www.skidmore.edu/dance
Skidmore College Office of Special Programs, www.skidmore.edu/odsp

NOTES

CHAPTER 1

1. "Public Diversions: From the Beginning Up to the Present Time," December 5, 1889, collection of the Saratoga Springs city historian.
2. Maria McBride Bucciferro, "Mogul of the Mob," *Saratoga Living* (Summer 2012).
3. Evelyn Barrett Britten, "Chronicles of Saratoga," July 1964, collection of the Saratoga Springs city historian.
4. 1894 Floral Fête souvenir booklet, Saratoga Room Collection, Saratoga Springs Public Library.
5. Teri Blasko and Jeff Durstwitz, "Long Ago and Far Away," *Mardi Gras Guide*, 2012.
6. "Grand Floral Ball," *Glens Falls Daily Times*, September 2, 1896, collection of the Saratoga Springs city historian.
7. *Troy Record*, September 6, 1901.
8. Blasko and Durstwitz, "Long Ago and Far Away."
9. Bucciferro, "Mogul of the Mob."
10. Mae Banner, "The Father of Dance in America," *Saratogian*, May 17, 1991.
11. Ruth St. Denis referred to herself as the "Goddess of Dance." She was a famous interpretive dancer who specialized in the exotic dance styles of the East. She and her partner, Ted Shawn, performed together as the Denishawn ensemble. Ted Shawn later formed a traveling group called the Men Dancers. He established the dance festival at Jacob's Pillow, his farm in Becket, Massachusetts. Ted Shawn is known as the "Father of American Dance."

12. http://www.nysparks.com/parks/saratogaspa.
13. *Saratogian*, "A History of the Saratoga County Fair," July 12, 2003, collection of the Saratoga Springs city historian.
14. *Saratogian*, "3,500 Attend Day Lily Festival in Congress Park," August 9, 1956, collection of the Saratoga Springs city historian.

CHAPTER 2

15. *Saratogian*, December 12, 1929.
16. Performance programs, Saratoga Room Collection, Saratoga Springs Public Library.
17. http://catalogue.skidmore.edu/content.php?catoid=6&navoid=222#History.
18. Isabel Brown interview, July 20, 2012.
19. Ibid.
20. Mary DiSanto-Rose interview, July 20, 2012.
21. http://www.skidmore.edu/dance/news.htm (all biographic information).
22. Eric Handman interview, November 3, 2012.
23. Debra J. Fernandez interview, August 24, 2012.
24. Rubén Graciani interview, October 1, 2012.
25. Mary DiSanto-Rose interview, July 20, 2012.
26. Marissa Maier, Backstage.com, September 28, 2012.

CHAPTER 3

27. *Saratogian*, "How to Succeed by Really Trying," *Performing Arts Saratoga '66* supplement, July 1966.
28. Timothy Holmes, *Saratoga Springs, New York: A Brief History* (Charleston, SC: The History Press, 2008), 106.
29. Newman E. Wait, *Saratoga Performing Arts Center Groundbreaking Program*, June 30, 1964.
30. "SPAC Our 40th Season," *Saratoga Performing Arts Center Commemorative Edition*, 2005.
31. Richard Leach, *Saratoga Performing Arts Center Groundbreaking Program*, June 30, 1964.
32. Nelson A. Rockefeller, governor, State of New York, *Saratoga Performing Arts Center Groundbreaking Program*, June 30, 1964.
33. Tina Lincer First, "Spell Is Still Strong for NYCB & Audience," *Saratoga Performing Arts Center 25th Anniversary Program*, 1990.

34. *Saratoga Performing Arts Center First Season Program*, 1966.
35. Edward and Carol Swyer interview, July 19, 2012.
36. BALANCHINE is a trademark of The George Balanchine Trust.
37. Lincoln Kirstein, *Thirty Years: The New York City Ballet* (New York: Alfred A. Knopf, 1978), 130.
38. Ibid., 217.
39. Ibid., 212.
40. Ibid., 191.
41. Leslie Roy-Heck interview, July 26, 2012.
42. Tina Lincer First, "Spell Is Still Strong for NYCB & Audience."
43. Ibid.
44. Ibid.
45. Andrew Wentink interview, July 21, 2012.
46. Kirstein, *Thirty Years*, 191.
47. Peter Martins interview, October 5, 2012.
48. Robert Maiorano interview, June 28, 2012.
49. Kay Leach interview, September 4, 2012.
50. Craig Claiborne, *New York Times*, February 23, 1983.
51. *Saratoga Performing Arts Center 25th Anniversary Program*, July 1990.
52. Robert Maiorano interview, June 28, 2012.
53. Mae G. Banner, "Saratoga Is Ballet Heaven," *Saratogian*, July 18, 1987.
54. Peter Martins interview, October 5, 2012.
55. Ed Lewi interview, July 30, 2012.
56. Sheila Parkert interview, August 15, 2012.
57. Daniel Duell interview, November 15, 2012.
58. Andrew Wentink interview, August 21, 2012.
59. Kay Leach interview, September 4, 2012.
60. Kathryn Levy interview, November 14, 2012.
61. Mayor Raymond Watkin interview, August 21, 2012.
62. Jennifer Dunning, "Saratoga Celebrates Balanchine," *New York Times*, July 16, 1977. BALANCHINE is a trademark of The George Balanchine Trust.
63. Mayor Raymond Watkin interview, August 21, 2012.
64. Ibid.
65. Herb Chesbrough, "In Our Opinion," *Saratogian*, October 1977.
66. Mayor Raymond Watkin interview, August 21, 2012.
67. Tina Lincer First, "Spell Is Still Strong for NYCB & Audience." *BALANCHINE is a trademark of The George Balanchine Trust.*
68. Peter Martins interview, October 5, 2012.
69. Ibid.
70. Mae Banner, "Carnival of the Animals," *Saratogian*, July 2003.
71. Mae Banner, "Symphony in Three Movements," *Saratogian*, July 2004.

72. Mae G. Banner, "Exquisite Gems–NYCB Dance," *Metroland on Line* 27, no. 30 (July 2004).
73. Jay Rogoff, "The New York City Ballet," *Saratogian*, July 14, 2012.
74. Alistair Macaulay, Dance Review, *New York Times*, July 18, 2012, C5.
75. Marcia White interview, August 30, 2012.
76. Ibid.
77. *Saratoga Performing Arts Center 40th Anniversary Program*, July 2005.
78. http://www.spac.org/aboutspac.cfm.
79. Edward Swyer interview, July 19, 2012.

CHAPTER 4

80. Advertisement of 1904, Saratoga Room Collection, Saratoga Springs Public Library.
81. Peggy Delay interview, August 29, 2012.
82. Ibid.
83. Ballerina Marina Svetlova had a summer ballet program in Dorset, Vermont, and regularly brought her students to the Saratoga Performing Arts Center to see the New York City Ballet performances.
84. In addition to the summer school, Briansky opened the Glens Falls Ballet and Dance Center, where future ballet teacher Patti Pugh was a student. Oleg Briansky and Mireille Briane interview, August 3, 2012.
85. CETA, the Comprehensive Employment and Training Act of the 1970s, was utilized by many nonprofit dance organizations as a temporary means of hiring their dancers and staff.
86. Phyllis Latin interview, July 20, 2012.
87. Christy Handley interview, September 29, 2012.
88. Aggie Jacobowsky for Michael Steele, interview July 15, 2012.
89. Dianne Carola interview, August 31, 2012.
90. Julie Gedalecia interview, July 25, 2012.
91. Leslie Roy-Heck interview, July 26, 2012.
92. The Otto family has produced several professional dancers, including siblings William, David, Philip and Deborah Otto.
93. David Otto interview, July 26, 2012.
94. Raul Martinez interview, July 26, 2012.
95. Leslie Roy-Heck interview, July 26, 2012.
96. https://myersnortheast.org.
97. Beth Fecteau interview, October 5, 2012.
98. Leslie Anne LaGuardia interview, August 26, 2012.
99. https://tangofusiondance.com.

100. Debra J. Fernandez interview, August 24, 2012.
101. Rhona Koretzky-Forman interview, August 21, 2012.
102. Peter Kobor interview, August 24, 2012.
103. Lincoln Kirstein, *Thirty Years of the New York City Ballet* (New York: Alfred A. Knopf, 1978), 47.
104. John Martin obituary, *Schenectady Gazette*, May 20, 1985.
105. Andrew Wentink interview, August 21, 2012.
106. Douglas Martin, "Cris Alexander Obituary," *New York Times*, March 24, 2012.
107. *Saratogian*, "Suzanne Ames Landry obituary," September 17, 2008.
108. Jennifer Dunning, "Anthony Blum Obituary," *New York Times*, February 6, 2000.
109. Robert Maiorano interview, June 28, 2012.
110. Leslie Roy-Heck interview, July 26, 2012.
111. Carl Landa interview, December 10, 2012.
112. Kim Vanyo interview, December 29, 2012.

Chapter 5

113. Mrs. Marylou Whitney through Heather Mabee interview, July 12, 2012.
114. *Webster's New World Collegiate Dictionary*, 4th ed. (Cleveland, OH: Wiley Publishing, Inc., 2008).
115. Edward and Carol Swyer interview, July 19, 2012.
116. Alison Moore interview, August 2, 2012.
117. Sharon Walsh interview, June 29, 2012.
118. Ibid.
119. Alison Moore interview, August 2, 2012.
120. Ibid.
121. Sharon Walsh interview, June 29, 2012.
122. Alison Moore interview, August 2, 2012.
123. Donna Skiff interview, July 11, 2012.
124. Heather Mabee interview, July 12, 2012.
125. Susan Edwards interview, November 18, 2012.
126. Ibid.
127. Alison Moore interview, August 2, 2012.
128. Heather Mabee interview, July 12, 2012.
129. Carol Swyer interview, July 19, 2012.
130. Michele Riggi interview, October 28, 2012.
131. Ibid.
132. Edward Swyer interview, July 19, 2012.

133. The American Craftsman style was an architectural design aesthetic popular from the late 1800s through 1930. The Washington Bath House was built in this style, as was the building for the Swyer Studios.

CHAPTER 6

134. Donald McCormack interview, August 2, 2011.
135. Sharon Arpey interview, July 25, 2012.
136. Ibid.

CHAPTER 7

137. Isabel Brown interview, July 20, 2012.
138. Saratoga Performing Arts Center, "SPAC Commemorative Edition," *Our 40th Season* program, July 2005.
139. Wendy Liberatore, *Daily Gazette*, June 2, 1991.
140. Mae G. Banner, review of Garth Fagan Dance Company, *Metroland*, 2006.
141. Ibid.

CHAPTER 8

142. Antoinette (Toni) Smith interview, October 25, 2012.
143. Rhona Koretzky-Forman interview, September 21, 2012.
144. Mary Ann Fantauzzi interview, June 29, 2012.
145. Ibid.
146. "Mission Statement of The Dance Alliance," *Saratoga Dances II Program*, October 20, 2012.
147. Mary Ann Fantauzzi interview, June 29, 2012.
148. *Apollo*, choreographed by George Balanchine. ©The George Balanchine Trust.
149. Justin Peck interview, October 22, 2012.
150. Antoinette (Toni) Smith interview, October 25, 2012.
151. http.//www.partnersindance.org.

CHAPTER 9

152. "Arts Education: The Commitment Continues," *Hudson Valley Magazine*, SPAC's 35th Season Commemorative Edition, July 2000.

153. Ibid.
154. https.//www.spac.org/aboutpage2.cfm.
155. Ibid.
156. https.//www.spac.org/action-council.cfm.
157. Antoinette Smith interview, October 25, 2012.
158. "Ballet Pre-Performance Talks," *SPAC 2012*, New York City Ballet program.
159. "SPAC Ballet Season Pre-Shows," *SPAC 2012*, New York City Ballet program.
160. BALANCHINE is a tademark of The George Balanchine Trust.
161. Peter Martins, with Howard Kaplan, *NYCB Workout* (New York: Quill/William Morrow and Company, 1997).
162. Mary Ann Fantauzzi interview, June 29, 2012.

CHAPTER 10

163. Mary Daly interview, July 10, 2012.
164. Carolyn Adams interview, August 8, 2011.
165. http://www.oce.nysed.gov/nysssaSOD.

CHAPTER 11

166. Sharon Arpey interview, July 25, 2012.
167. https://saratogaartsfest.org.
168. Sharon Arpey interview, July 25, 2012.
169. Debra Fernandez interview, August 24, 2012.
170. http://danceflurry.org.
171. http://www.yaddo.org/yaddo/history.shtml.
172. http://www.nyra.com/index_saratoga.html.

CHAPTER 12

173. "35 Seasons of Ballet," *Hudson Valley Magazine*, SPAC's 35th Season Commemorative Edition, 2000, p. 17.
174. Kay Leach interview, September 4, 2012.
175. Sheila Parkert interview, August 15, 2012.
176. Mary Ann Fantauzzi interview, June 29, 2012.
177. Christie Handley interview, Septmenber 29, 2012.
178. Rhona Koretzky-Forman interview, September 21, 2012.
179. Martins with Kaplan, *NYCB Workout*.
180. Mary Ann Fantauzzi interview, June 29, 2012.

181. Christie Handley interview, September 29, 2012.
182. *In G Major*, choreography by George Balanchine, ©The George Balanchine Trust.
183. Rhona Koretzky-Forman interview, September 21, 2012.
184. Susan Edwards interview, November 18, 2012.
185. Saratoga Performing Arts Center, New York City Ballet Program, July 1991, 63.
186. Ibid., 64.
187. Donald McCormack interview, August 2, 2012.
188. Jay Rogoff interview, November 2, 2012.
189. Jay Rogoff, *The Art of Gravity* (New Orleans: Louisiana State University Press, 2011); *Hopkins Review*, Johns Hopkins University Press; *Ballet Review*, http://www.balletreview.com.
190. Michele and Ronald Riggi interview, October 28, 2012.
191. Rhona Koretzky-Forman interview, September 21, 2012.
192. Mayor Raymond Watkin interview, August 21, 2012.
193. Shawn Banner interview, July 23, 2012.
194. Marcia White and Peter Martins, Saratoga Performing Arts Center press release, July 2007.

Bibliography

Bucciferro, Harry. "Saratoga Heritage." *Saratoga Living* (Summer 2011).

Golnick, Arthur. "Generations in Balance." *Simply Saratoga.* Saratoga Springs, NY: Saratoga Publishing, LLC, n.d.

Holmes, Timothy. *Saratoga Springs: A Brief History*. Charleston, SC: The History Press, 2008.

Kirstein, Lincoln. *Thirty Years: The New York City Ballet*. New York: Alfred A. Knopf, Inc., 1973.

Maiorano, Robert. *Worlds Apart.* Reading, PA: Aperture Press, 1980.

McBride, Maria. "Mogul of the Mob." *Saratoga Living* (Summer 2012).

Seymour, Maurice, with Leonide, Massine, Pelligrini and Cudahy. *Seymour on Ballet.* Chicago, 1947.

Terry, Walter. *The Dance in America.* New York: Harper and Row, 1971.

Websites

www.dancealliance.org

www.dancemuseum.org

www.nycballet.com

www.skidmore.edu

www.spac.org

About the Author

Denise Warner Limoli is a master ballet teacher who specializes in staging the nineteenth- and early twentieth-century ballet repertoire. As a featured dancer with American Ballet Theatre, she performed internationally with many of the world's greatest dancers. Ms. Warner Limoli was ballet master for several professional companies and was faculty in the dance departments of the University of Cincinnati College-Conservatory of Music and the North Carolina School of the Arts. She is a regular teacher for the American Ballet Theatre Summer Intensive Program, Kaatsbaan International Dance Center and the Nutmeg Conservatory. Denise Warner Limoli is associate professor of dance at Skidmore College and serves on the board of directors for the National Museum of Dance. She lives in Saratoga Springs, New York, with her husband, Michael Limoli, a musician and former dancer, and their two adult children.

Visit us at
www.historypress.net

This title is also available as an e-book